Past Masters
General Editor Keith Thomas

Goethe

Past Masters

AQUINAS Anthony Kenny
ARISTOTLE Jonathan Barnes
BACH Denis Arnold
FRANCIS BACON Anthony Quinton
BAYLE Elisabeth Labrousse
BERKELEY J. O. Urmson
THE BUDDHA Michael Carrithers
BURKE C. B. Macpherson
CARLYLE A. L. Le Quesne
CHAUCER George Kane
CLAUSEWITZ Michael Howard
COBBETT Raymond Williams
COLERIDGE Richard Holmes
CONFUCIUS Raymond Dawson
DANTE George Holmes
DARWIN Jonathan Howard
DIDEROT Peter France
GEORGE ELIOT Rosemary Ashton
ENGELS Terrell Carver
GALILEO Stillman Drake

GOETHE T. J. Reed
HEGEL Peter Singer
HOMER Jasper Griffin
HUME A. J. Ayer
JESUS Humphrey Carpenter
KANT Roger Scruton
LAMARCK L. J. Jordanova
LEIBNIZ G. MacDonald Ross
LOCKE John Dunn
MACHIAVELLI Quentin Skinner
MARX Peter Singer
MENDEL Vitezslav Orel
MONTAIGNE Peter Burke
THOMAS MORE Anthony Kenny
WILLIAM MORRIS Peter Stansky
MUHAMMAD Michael Cook
NEWMAN Owen Chadwick
PASCAL Alban Krailsheimer
PETRARCH Nicholas Mann
PLATO R. M. Hare
PROUST Derwent May
TOLSTOY Henry Gifford

Forthcoming

AUGUSTINE Henry Chadwick
BERGSON Leszek Kolakowski
JOSEPH BUTLER R. G. Frey
CERVANTES P. E. Russell
COPERNICUS Owen Gingerich
DESCARTES Tom Sorell
DISRAELI John Vincent
ERASMUS James McConica
GIBBON J. W. Burrow
GODWIN Alan Ryan
HERZEN Aileen Kelly
JEFFERSON Jack P. Greene
JOHNSON Pat Rogers
KIERKEGAARD Patrick Gardiner
LEONARDO E. H. Gombrich
LINNAEUS W. T. Stearn

MILL William Thomas
MONTESQUIEU Judith Shklar
NEWTON P. M. Rattansi
ROUSSEAU Robert Wokler
RUSKIN George P. Landow
RUSSELL John G. Slater
SHAKESPEARE Germaine Greer
ADAM SMITH D. D. Raphael
SOCRATES Bernard Williams
SPINOZA Roger Scruton
VICO Peter Burke
VIRGIL Jasper Griffin
WYCLIF Anthony Kenny

and others

T. J. Reed

Goethe

Oxford   New York

OXFORD UNIVERSITY PRESS

1984

Oxford University Press, Walton Street, Oxford OX2 6DP

London New York Toronto
Delhi Bombay Calcutta Madras Karachi
Kuala Lumpur Singapore Hong Kong Tokyo
Nairobi Dar es Salaam Cape Town
Melbourne Auckland

and associated companies in
Beirut Berlin Ibadan Mexico City Nicosia

Oxford is a trade mark of Oxford University Press

First published 1984 as an Oxford University Press paperback
and simultaneously in a hardback edition

British Library Cataloguing in Publication Data

Reed, T. J.
Goethe.—(Past masters)
1.Goethe, Johann Wolfgang von—Criticism
and interpretation
I. Title II. Series
838'.609   PT2177
ISBN 0-19-287503-5
ISBN 0-19-287502-7 Pbk

Library of Congress Cataloging in Publication Data

Reed, T. J. (Terence James), 1937–
Goethe
(Past masters)
Includes index.
1. Goethe, Johann Wolfgang von, 1749–1832.
2. Authors, German—18th century—Biography.   3. Authors,
German—19th century—Biography.   I. Title.
II. Series
PT2049.R4 1984 831'.6[B] 84-5702
ISBN 0-19-287503-5
ISBN 0-19-287502-7 (pbk.)

Set by Hope Services, Abingdon
Printed in Great Britain by
St. Edmundsbury Press Ltd
Bury St. Edmunds, Suffolk

Contents

Note on references   *vi*

INTRODUCTION   *1*

1   INDIVIDUAL   *8*
    Poetry   *8*
    Werther   *17*
    Drama   *22*

2   ORDER   *29*
    Weimar   *29*
    Italy   *32*
    Love   *40*
    Science   *43*

3   CLASSICISM   *54*

4   *FAUST*   *66*

5   VARIATIONS   *82*

6   'A HAPPY CONSTELLATION'   *94*

Note on Sources   *103*

Further Reading   *106*

Index   *111*

Note on references

References within the text are to the following sources:

H   the Hamburg Edition of Goethe's works in 14 volumes, edited by Erich Trunz; original impression, Hamburg 1948–60.

E   Goethe's conversations as recorded, with dates, in the last decade of his life by his amanuensis Johann Peter Eckermann.

D   Goethe's diary of the journey from Karlsbad to Rome in autumn 1786 (not in H).

Goethe's letters are referred to by date only. Most of those quoted can be found in the four-volume selection edited by Karl Robert Mandelkow, Hamburg 1962–7, uniform with the Hamburg Edition of the works.

Sources for the quotations from other writers are given on pp. 103–5.

Introduction

Goethe's name inspires for the most part only a vague respect in the English-speaking world. He is known to be a pinnacle of European literature, 'Gouty' alongside 'Daunty' and 'Shopkeeper' in James Joyce's three-man poetic firm. But to many English readers it is no longer clear why, though they may be aware that he wrote a famous *Faust*. In the nineteenth century it was different. The English Romantics knew Goethe's work and recognised his achievement, individual and national. Byron addressed him as 'first of existing writers, who has created the literature of his own country and illustrated that of Europe'. Goethe had provided models for some of Byron's dramatic work and a major stimulus for Scott's historical novels. By 1830 he was an established name in Britain, despite some reputation among the less open-minded for blasphemy and immorality. (Coleridge resisted the temptation to translate *Faust*, fearing guilt-by-association.) For the more cosmopolitan Victorians—Carlyle, Matthew Arnold, George Eliot—Goethe was unquestionably a major force in the shaping of modern culture, a touchstone for contemporary greatness and 'the Wisest of our Time' (Carlyle).

This last was insidious praise. When the nineteenth-century tradition of firsthand contact with German culture was lost, wisdom—not the most immediately exciting of literary qualities—was what remained of Goethe's repute. It attached itself to that other uninviting creation of the nineteenth century, Goethe the cultural monument. In his later lifetime, travelling notables had called on him in Weimar and left accounts of their encounters with the 'Olympian'—his grand manner on these stiff occasions must surely have owed a good deal to embarrassment. The lesser mortals of his entourage recorded and subsequently published their conversations with him in his later years. His pronouncements, sometimes all too plainly induced ('I asked Goethe what he thought about . . .') came to seem part of the corpus of his work, apodictic and firm beside the more fluid utterances of poetry.

Then, from the last decades of the century on, German academics in the new specialised career of 'Goethe philology' laboured devotedly to organise the vast materials of his life and works: the great editions, the innumerable records and reports, the fifteen thousand letters. But they avoided and even discouraged open discussion of the literary values which their activity presupposed. To the outside observer, Goethe was a dignified national possession half-hidden behind a scaffolding of scholarship, a long row of leatherbound volumes in the bourgeois bookcase. Reverence was the premiss, and unquestioned reverence can block the live flow of communication with a writer's work. The flow is still not restored in Germany, where the rigid positions of the past are blamed on the poet himself. Meanwhile outside Germany the dominant image is still that of the ponderous sage of Weimar. It is an image of stasis and age, not of creative vigour: 'gouty' indeed.

Yet what marks Goethe out in every phase of his long life is an essentially youthful creativity, a gift for starting afresh time and again with new materials and a new impulse, what he himself called 'repeated puberty' and 'sloughing off skins' (E 11 March 1828; H 1.324). Inspiration and spontaneity returned without fail. If he became an 'old' public figure, and eventually also in some measure a sage, he stayed a 'young' poet. When he fell in love yet again at seventy-four with a girl aged seventeen, and on losing her wrote one of his finest poems, a massive and majestic elegy bitterly rejecting all the hard-won principles on which his latter years were built, it was only an extreme instance of the way he could cast off habit and create new form. He lived by self-renewal, going beyond each rounded achievement to find himself again in a new world, shaping his experience in a sequence of ethical and aesthetic modes any one of which was enough to make a lasting reputation. Each adds some-thing substantial to our picture not just of Goethe but of man and his place, extends the range of formal virtuosity, opens up new depths of psychological probing, taps new sources—Germanic, Graeco-Roman, Persian, Chinese, humanistic, scientific—of cultural enrichment.

So for sixty years, from 1770 till his death in 1832, Goethe's development was the centre of a German national literature which he raised, largely through his own accomplishments but also through his inspiration, from an uncertain infancy and dependence on foreign models to a point where it was felt to be the main spiritual energy of Europe; so much so that even a culture as insular and accustomed to supremacy as that of France sought new stimulus from it.

The medium of Goethe's explorations may be verse or prose, drama, novel or poem, scientific or aesthetic essay or travel record, autobiography or letter. For him each is a means dictated by the occasion and the experience he is responding to, often taken up unplanned under the immediate stress of that experience. He is not, as the specialised professional writer is, committed to 'litera-ture' as such or to any one of its forms. The production of his next novel or play is rarely an end in itself. He is not writing primarily for the market. The overriding aim is self-expression and communication. In the autobiography *Poetry and Truth* (*Dichtung und Wahrheit*) he called his works 'fragments of a great confession' (H 9.283), and it has since been a truism to speak of him as a confessional writer. But equally important in that famous formulation is the idea that works are inescapably fragments—that is, that even the most perfect forms remain partial achievements within the complex continuum of a life.

Not that Goethe was careless of form. He set great store by formal perfection, frequently pursued it with extreme deliberateness and sophistication, and just as frequently achieved it (especially in his poetry) with demonstrable effortlessness. In his Classical phase he raised form to a supreme principle, and jointly with Schiller he did more than any previous German writer to secure the status of literary works as privileged utterances which cannot be simplistically impugned on moral, doctrinal or legal grounds. Yet in the last analysis he still does not detach form from life as an absolute value. Art remained for him unquestionably in the service of life, just as it depended on life for its impulse and material. To the last he insisted that 'the substance of poetry is the substance of our own life' (H 12.361). So although Goethe is very far from being a conventional moralist, his writings are in the broadest sense ethical and not merely aesthetic in their allegiance.

His outward life is quickly sketched. Johann Wolfgang Goethe was born in 1749 in the Free Imperial City of Frankfurt am Main. His father was a well-to-do bourgeois, trained in the law, and an Imperial Counsellor. His mother was a woman of outstanding vivacity and shrewd sense, much esteemed later as an acquaintance and correspondent by the writers and princes with whom her son's fame brought her into contact. Her letters have the same overflowing spontaneous individuality as his, and he was to say that his 'happy nature' and pleasure in the imagination were an inheritance from her (H 1.320). Just as important, her loving care was the deepest source of that sense of being at home in life that shaped all his work.

After studying law in Leipzig and Strasbourg, Goethe briefly practised in his home city. In 1775, on the strength of his reputation as author of a successful play and a sensational novel, he was invited to visit Carl August, Duke of Saxe-Weimar. The visit lasted: Weimar became Goethe's base for the rest of his life. In the first decade there he was burdened with administrative labours (he had not been asked to stay on merely as a court poet) and he carried them out with as much efficiency and compassion as the system allowed. In 1786 he escaped from these duties and other problems and indulged in prolonged truancy in Italy, drawing and studying. This idyllic period was the happiest of his life and it revolutionised his vision of art and existence. He returned to Weimar having negotiated freer terms, no longer a full-time administrator although still decidedly a beneficiary of feudal patronage—in this respect too he was independent of the literary market.

The waves of history rarely washed into his Weimar backwater. He travelled with the German princes' army which failed to defeat revolutionary France and restore the monarchy in 1792. Otherwise he moved only to visit Switzerland or the spas of Bohemia. The years of 'High Classicism', of which he was co-founder, coincided with a separate peace that took the North German states out of the Revolutionary and Napoleonic Wars. But in 1806 the renewal of war caught up with him when French troops flooded through Weimar after the battle of Jena. (His long-established mistress Christiane Vulpius safeguarded his household, and he was moved to marry her.) As Carl August's adviser he knew political realities at the level of the German mini-state, he met some of the principal figures in the Europe of his day, spoke with Napoleon and Metternich; but he never had political influence in the larger context. 'Statesman' would be a misnomer.

The first half of Goethe's life coincided with the later Enlightenment. Though he is not usually thought of as part of it, its principles are present in his work as an unspoken foundation: empiricism, attachment to the sensuous world, intellectual independence and secularism, confidence in man's nature and particularly in his own, a forthright clarity of thought. If he said little about these things as principles, that is because he was busy living them and charging them with the vitality of his personal mode of vision and experience. Against this background, the main event of Goethe's intellectual life in his early years was the encounter in Strasbourg with Johann Gottfried Herder, whose philosophy of culture perfectly accommodated and confirmed the young poet's creative impulses and thematic interests. The first years in Weimar stimulated Goethe's interest in science, and for the rest of his life science was a major preoccupation and a complement—in a very integral sense—to hi' poetic work. Then in his middle years came the friendshi; with Friedrich Schiller, himself a great poet and tragic dramatist, and also a brilliant aesthetic theorist and critic. His perception and description of Goethe's poetic nature and its unique value in modern Europe added a dimension to Goethe's awareness and gave his creativity new impetus. The two men's highly productive partnership between 1794 and Schiller's death in 1805 provided Germany with a belated Classicism and, for the first time, a centre of literary authority, Weimar. Young writers were drawn there, especially the members of what became the self-consciously new 'Romantic' group. Goethe remained cautious in his dealings with them, aware that their praise of his work and affinities with his thought masked deeper divergences of outlook and poetic aims. After Schiller's death he was left essentially alone, known to the whole of Europe but lacking intimates of stature, living in and for his art and science. His intellectual activity was unabated, his lyrical poetry still flowing, the drama *Faust* and his autobiography only just completed, when he died in March 1832, halfway through his eighty-third year.

1 Individual

Poetry

Goethe is above all else a poet. He was the first to
explore fully (which means that he virtually created) the
expressive registers of modern German. His phrasing,
cadences and rhythms mark out the emotional bounds
of the language and establish its poetic character as
Shakespeare's do for English and Pushkin's for Russian.
They are part of the national consciousness and the
stock of near-proverbial formulations. Along with Luther's
Bible translation, they helped create the German cultural identity.

That is for present purposes a problem. Since the finest
poetry does not readily translate, how can Goethe's
literary achievement be suggested? No English version
has yet managed to render adequately the feel of his
poems or (despite many attempts) of his *Faust*, which
lives by the power and beauty of characteristic poetic
speech rather than by strictly dramatic qualities. Even
so, the vital effect of Goethe's poetry is not wholly shut
away in an unfamiliar language or the history of a
foreign culture. Though its immediate texture cannot be
conveyed, the conceptions and responses which make
the substance of the poems can be, and they are exciting
and exemplary enough. They too are in their way
historic, but fit into a familiar pattern: the situation in
which the poems arise, and their relation to the modes
they replace, are part of a process that began all over
Europe in the late eighteenth century. In that broad
context, Goethe—certainly the young Goethe—is a

8

Romantic. Nevertheless, he cannot be fully assimilated into that movement. The light he casts on it, on its problems and its immense historical aftermath, is distinctive and radically challenging.

Young poets have to begin somewhere; usually they follow the fashions that prevail around them. For a while, as a student at Leipzig, Goethe plays at poetry as a party-game, writes elegant banalities about maidens, zephyrs, groves and stolen kisses. But meantime his letters are already expressing a personality too vigorous to be contained for long by rococo artifice. This real voice of the letters breaks into his poetry in the early seventies, in Strasbourg. Or rather, around Strasbourg, because the crucial thing now and for the rest of his life is the reality of the natural world that meets and matches his vigour of feeling and keenness of perception. He experiences the external world through avid senses, and his response becomes the shape of his poems.

Eighteenth-century poetry before this had largely been cooped up in the drawing-room of social emotions or the schoolroom of received doctrines. If it looked out of the windows, it was only at the tamed nature to be found in orderly gardens. Its formal patterns were similarly restricted: 'lyrical' stanzas jingled, earnest disquisitions plodded, fables tried to lighten the journey towards predictable conclusions, rhyme and rhythm did as they were told. Only one earlier German poet, Klopstock, had tried to free himself with grandiose verbal and rhythmic gestures. But his poems (as the great critic Lessing said) are so filled with feeling that it is often hard to feel anything when reading them. The emotions are too actively induced, and they assail us with a demanding rhetoric. They are also often specifically religious emotions, a 'sublime' intensification of the same Christian

9

orthodoxy which had for so long set limits to poetic expression, and were thus a dubious liberation.

Goethe, by contrast, escapes fully into the real world about him. It is an escape which poetry had in a sense been looking forward to since long before his century. From Roman times poets had intermittently appealed against the forced formality of social life, its great houses and artificial gardens with their 'adulterous' graftings, and pointed to the open fields where (in Andrew Marvell's words) 'willing nature does to all dispense/ A wild and fragrant innocence'. But they had scarcely gone out into that so enticingly evoked realm to explore it. Even the precociously modern Petrarch, who 'wandered free and alone among the mountains, forests and streams', did not do so for long without being troubled by theological objections to such a concern with earthly things; and he certainly did not introduce these realities into the stylised world of his poetry. There was only one tradition in which the countryside necessarily figured, namely pastoral. But at least until the late eighteenth century, it stylised the realities of nature (not to mention country labour) out of existence altogether.

Goethe does what his timorous predecessors had not. He becomes consciously a 'wanderer', moving through what he variously calls 'the free world', 'the full world', 'the open world'; and the rhythms of his movement as he trudges across muddy fields in the pouring rain, or rides through the Alsace countryside to a lovers' meeting, or is rowed in a boat on Lake Zurich, are directly felt in his poetry. Few other poets draw us so powerfully into their specific experience and so enrich the emotional with the physical. Goethe is a real presence in natural surroundings which he makes equally real through intense and exact perceptions—dusk hanging on the mountains, darkness looking out like eyes from among the foliage of trees, stars of sunlight winking on morning wave-crests—but above all (since no description can fully capture reality) through the evocation of his matching response, so that we know what it felt like to be that individual, there, then. The poems grow out of a particular occasion in the poet's life, wholly personal yet also (it turns out) wholly communicable. Where the term 'occasional poem' had previously meant the most deliberate rhetorical treatment of a public theme—the battles and birthdays of the powerful—it came to mean for Goethe the new poetic process of giving spontaneous expression to a distinctive experience (H 10.48; 13.39).

This approach brings conventional poetic modes vividly and unconventionally to life. Like no other spring poem before it, Goethe's 'Maifest' (May Festival) links the energies that thrust upwards through earth, branches and the throats of birds with the answering exclamations that thrust up within the poet, excited, uninhibited, naïve in a positive sense. The traditional lovers' meeting is similarly renewed: the poet rides out into the evening countryside, we see with his eyes as he forges through the dusk, and the patterns of objects and spaces moving before him people his imagination with monsters. When the lovers have met, and parted, we share his view of her through tears as she turns away—I follow the authentic unrevised version of the poem 'Willkommen und Abschied' (Welcome and Parting)—and are caught up in the affirmation that grows as an immediate response to momentary sorrow: that, pain and all, to be loved and above all to love is an overriding good fortune.

In both these poems the form is entirely regular. Yet there is no sense of rhetorical arrangement, only of necessary expression; no sense that language, verse, stanza are imposing any kind of restraint on the flow and connection of ideas and feeling. A new force has been infused into traditional forms. Or rather, the sense of form as a chosen container, which dominated previous German poetry, has yielded to the sense of form as a garment shaping itself to the body of thought and emotion—or, better still, as itself the body into which thought and emotion have grown. This is even more apparent where the form is improvised and innovative, unique to the single occasion. True to T. S. Eliot's dictum that there is no separate entity 'free verse', only good verse, bad verse, and chaos, Goethe's 'free' verse takes firm and functionally necessary shape around the movements of his mind: for example, in 'Prometheus', which re-enacts the hero's proud independence of Zeus by its defiant verbal and rhythmic gestures; or in the complementary myth of 'Ganymed', where quite different rhythms convey the ecstatic flow towards the boy's mystical union with Zeus/Nature; or in 'An Schwager Kronos' (To Coachman Kronos) which catches the jolting motion of an eighteenth-century coach-ride, straining slowly uphill and careering downhill, and keeps this very physical feel even as it becomes a new-coined myth for the triumphal journey through life of a favoured being. In these and other vigorous hymnic poems, there is no arbitrariness in phrasing, sense-grouping or line-breaks. The creative *fait accompli* is persuasive in every detail, the movements of the mind pattern the words and rhythms as a magnet patterns iron-filings.

Everywhere the poet speaks with a frank and seemingly artless voice. This is in the fullest sense of Wordsworth's phrase 'a man speaking to men'. Yet the formal results are anything but rustic and simple. It is as if Goethe only needs to say what he sees and does, what he thinks and feels, for poetry to take its own perfect shape. Poems which we know from the clearest evidence arose quite unpremeditated and at once, needing no 'recollection of emotion in tranquillity', prove to have a coherence of detail, a subtle correspondence between their changing movement and the phases in a sequence of emotions, and an overall symmetry which might seem the work of supreme craft. They are not verbal constructs but verbal organisms, shaped at deeper levels of the poet's mind than that of the conscious act of composing. Later poets and critics in their cool laboratories have scorned the idea of 'inspiration'. But there is no apter word for those moments when, through no act of will, a complex of thought and feeling comes suddenly together in a human mind and takes clear and compelling form.

For all this vigour, freshness and poetic precision, there are no German antecedents and few later equals. They had, it is true, their prophet: Herder, whom Goethe met at just this time (1771) in Strasbourg, preached the naturalness of primitive peoples and their song, the primal power of Homer, Ossian (!) and more recently Shakespeare. Did Herder influence Goethe? Some accounts almost make him jointly responsible for this first creative burst. Certainly he set Goethe off collecting and ultimately imitating Alsace folksong—if 'imitating' is an adequate word for the process that produced poems like 'Heidenröslein' (Rose on the Heath), 'Erlkönig' (Erl-King), or Gretchen's songs of love and loss in *Faust*. But no amount of preachment and influence can create creativity. In any case, to a rising poet cultural theories and exhortation must be less vital than actual literary models— Shakespeare, whom Goethe read long

13

before he met Herder; or Pindar, whose complex metres he misunderstood excitingly as an invitation to rhapsodic effusion; or Klopstock, whose example then seemed fresh and inspiring. Everything we know about the way Goethe worked makes it unlikely that as he wrote he was consciously fulfilling a scheme of cultural renewal. At most, the contact with Herder and his ideas may have strengthened Goethe's sense of licence to be himself, in the ultimate cause of poetry. For the rest, he was what he was, of nobody's making, a fortunate fulfilment of what Herder was hoping for.

The gift of 'being himself' is crucial. Any independent vision has to assert itself against the pressures of the past, still deadeningly alive in the present—half of the present *is* the past, the other half is the shapeable future. If Goethe's vision of nature and man seems obvious and right to us now, that is only because he asserted it so fully and successfully. To see and state the obvious was a creative achievement, then. 'The art of seeing nature', as John Constable later wrote, 'is a thing almost as much to be acquired as the art of reading the Egyptian hieroglyphics.' Goethe's reading of the world was so much his own that he later spoke of it as something innate, an 'anticipation' of reality which made experience superfluous or even a disturbance (H 10.431; E 26 Feb. 1824). But this is a slightly fanciful extreme. Everything he says at the time has a strong flavour of empiricism. Frequently he is opposing his own earthly self-sufficiency of being and perception to the otherworldliness of the orthodox. To Christian friends he speaks of himself as a 'very earthly man', made up of 'the truth of the five senses', content to 'dwell in himself'—a condition which he calls 'the best happiness' (28 Oct. 1779; 8 June 1774). He is, as a humorous poem seriously says, a 'child of this world' hemmed in by prophets (H 1.90). Poetry, he was to write much later, is a 'worldly gospel' (H 9.580). The young Goethe consciously enters into the heritage of a secular reality.

This fundamental self-confidence is a large part of his literary character. Though it would have meant little—for us—without the matching power of expression that made him a poet, the gift of words would not have made him the poet he is without his intense attachment to the world, the earthy independence of 'Prometheus' and the pantheistic devotion of 'Ganymed'. Nor was the attachment to the world just an exploitable poetic subject. Goethe is not on a visit among nature, half-turning already like many poets before and since to point a lesson and rush back with a completed poem into the safety of civilisation. In nature he finds his real roots, he intuits the one great system that embraces him along with all other living things. In the most striking of all his images, he is the child enclosed in nature's womb, sucking nourishment through the umbilical cord (H 1.102). Spring and autumn poems celebrate love as one of the forces of nature; they link human joy and sorrow literally with natural growth. This is not the 'pathetic fallacy', because for Goethe it is not fallacious: there is a real and benevolent continuity of nature and man. The poem written on Lake Zurich and later called 'Auf dem See' (On the Lake) resolves an inner crisis and ends in a vision of ripening fruit reflected in the water: two processes of maturing intertwine, not as a poetic conceit or decorative arabesque but as related manifestations of a common force. This means that the feeling of outward movement, of escape and exploration in these youthful poems is balanced by a sense of homecoming, an idyllic return. Goethe is not just a man writing *about* nature, he is a man discovering himself *as* nature. Romanticism was later to make the connection between man and nature a truism, even a platitude. But few Romantic poets manage to embody that truth (as distinct from merely declaring it) with such zest and consistency and so little solemnity as Goethe does.

His return to nature is also a very positive thing. It is quite unlike the bitter reaction that drove Rousseau out of town in search of country compensation. The young Goethe was a happy man and poet, and this too was a fulfilment. For most eighteenth-century thinkers, all was officially right with the world. What theology had always maintained in defence of God's design was now declared as a secular truth: the large patterns of life and history were meaningful and good. Enlightened optimism required Whatever Was to be Right, the world to be the best of all possible worlds. The secular argument for this was shakier than the theological—there was just as much evil in the world to gainsay it, and no longer any guarantor of ultimate coherence. Not surprisingly, whatever philosophers, divines or poets might say, there were few ebulliently happy men among them to bear witness in the very texture of their works to the ideal Rightness about which they theorised. (Paradoxically, the sceptic David Hume seems closer to contentment.) But Goethe does just this, not by argument or theory, which he does not yet have, but on the immediate grounds of felt experience. All's right with the world, at least within the scope of perception and feeling that his poems record.

This must not be understood trivially. Goethe's personal life had its difficulties, his temperament was not unproblematically sunny. His Leipzig studies were interrupted by some kind of nervous collapse and spiritual crisis, which precipitated him on his return home into a phase of intense pietism. He continued after his recovery to be a man carrying a high charge; his emotions could be turbulent, often dangerously so. His character struck others as volatile, his own sense of instability made him speak of himself as a chameleon. Yet beneath and beyond all particular difficulties, a sense persisted that there were answering energies in him that could cope; that life was inherently valuable and good; that the world (at least in its basic natural constituents) was benevolent. This almost physical confidence was to find larger reasons later, turning intuition into a consciously normative statement of order.

Werther

The young Goethe's optimistic individualism—the world validated on the pulses of sensuous man—is remote from tragedy, and remoter still from the axiom that life in itself is tragic. But it was not a philosophy beyond questioning or immune to accident. The individual wholly dependent on himself might go astray, circumstances might work on a vulnerable character, the very freedom from tutelage could put a human being at risk. The poignancy of such an aberration, unlike the almost routine downfalls that spring from the axiomatically tragic view, would be the greater for the assumption that life normally offers fulfilment.

Goethe did not actually choose to explore the theme for its literary possibilities. The task was forced on him by the suicide of Carl Wilhelm Jerusalem, a young lawyer whom he had known in Leipzig and at the Imperial Court of Appeal in Wetzlar. Natural death, even premature or accidental death, helps to define life; suicide

[margin notes: Optimism / Sensuous man]

[margin notes: Independence / Risky]

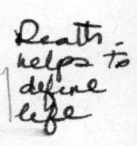

[margin note: Death - helps to define life]

17

questions its value. The self-destruction of someone he knew set Goethe the problem of comprehending such despair. Reports of Jerusalem's social failures, unhappy love, gruesomely mismanaged end and frugal burial shook and moved him. For eighteen months he digested them, then in four weeks early in 1774 wrote the epistolary novel *The Sufferings of Young Werther (Die Leiden des jungen Werthers)*, a story of inner turmoil and unrequited passion driving irresistibly to that dark end.

Werther's letters (after a brief 'editorial' note we hear no other voice till near the close) are the real thing as no previous eighteenth-century novelist had used it. What in Richardson and Rousseau had been letters often only in name, and a clumsy vehicle of narration, becomes in Goethe's hands a means to mime an authentic inner life. Each letter is an emotional phase, each is wholly plausible. Their style, the circumstances in which Werther writes them, their varying length and tone, their gradually crumbling coherence—everything feels real. We are drawn into the fluctuations of feeling as we are drawn into Goethe's poems, only now the expressive writing is conscious artifice, recreating a mental world which Goethe has imaginatively entered. When finally the Editor, whose appeal for our sympathies prefaced the letters, returns to report on Werther's last days and hours, borrowing particulars from Jerusalem's death in a harrowing montage, the sense of reality is further intensified. The terse 'objective' narration is an obvious foil to the subjective pathos of the letters; but it also serves to heighten that pathos, setting off Werther's last utterances to maximum effect.

The effect on the book's first readers was overwhelming and is legendary. The novel inspired not just emotion but emulation, in a wave of suicides similarly costumed,

blue coat, yellow waistcoat. Even without these real
sequels, the effect was inappropriate, and it continued to
be so for a long time. When the novel came out, people
who knew Jerusalem took it, understandably, for 'the
truth' about him. But Goethe had also lent the case some
emotional substance of his own, drawing on his unrequited love for an engaged girl in Wetzlar. This real   *Love*
Charlotte and her husband Kestner were now embar-
rassed that acquaintances who had seen Goethe much in
their company would take Werther's adoration of the
fictional Lotte, and every other detail of the novel's tragic
triangle, for 'the truth' about them. Later, as Goethe's
fame crowded out these lesser reputations, the novel
was taken to be the all-but-truth about him and the
straits to which love for Lotte had brought him: for the
biographistic nineteenth century, he had written it so as   *Suicide?*
not to commit suicide himself.

All these versions dissolve literature into fact, on the
philistine assumption that there is only fiction *or* fact,
poetry *or* truth. But the novel is poetry *and* truth, an
essential truth freed by fiction from the limitations of any
one real life and added to the store of human understanding. Goethe's fiction offers insight, or rather empathy,   *Insight*
into mental processes that can lead to death as inexorably   *empathy*
as a bodily disease. Werther uses that parallel himself in
defending suicides against the conventional views of his
rival, Lotte's fiancé Albert, long before his own resolve
to die is taken. His eloquence makes explicit the
revolutionary appeal for understanding which contrasts
with rigid law and morals. It stands beside Hume's essay
Of Suicide, written long before but cautiously withheld
and only published three years after *Werther*. But where
Hume argues abstractly for a man's right to kill himself,
Goethe recreates concretely the sufferings that may drive

him to it. Philosophy invites generalised assent, literature compels an initially specific compassion. That is its distinctive approach to the task of civilising society.

Werther's sufferings come not just from unhappy love, although romantic emotion dominates the surface plot and is intensified by every means short of mawkishness (at least by the standards of the day). At a deeper level Werther needs Lotte as an answer, or palliative, to more radical problems. His love for her absorbs a mind which, left to itself, runs on transience and death. He sees human activity as ultimately pointless, as a restriction from which he, the brooding observer outside society, is free—but free in a nihilistic wilderness. So he also yearns for some form of the restriction he scorns: in the idyllic setting of the book's opening, he could wish to be a peasant, so busy and fulfilled that when the leaves fall he would think no more than that winter is coming. The idyll is destroyed piece by piece; Lotte, the perfect partner for a true idyll, is unobtainable. Werther loses all sense of his own value, his pleasures turn bitter, nature the source of ecstatic happiness becomes nature the all-devouring monster. Meaning finally drains from life. The condition is not new: it is the medieval *taedium vitae*, the melancholy and hypochondria widely discussed in the seventeenth and eighteenth centuries. But in Werther it is more acute and all-embracing; and it throws up images that will dominate modern pessimism—man as a helpless puppet, the abyss, the senseless repetition of rising and going to bed again.

Nothing, it seems, could be more different from the zest and affirmation of the poems Goethe had written and was still writing. Was *Werther* merely a 'saison en enfer', a sacrifice to the demands of the empathetic imagination, a challenge to his own serenity, reminding us that art is not a risk-free activity? In part, no doubt, the chameleon artist was deliberately taking on the spiritual colour of his subject, entertaining Werther's thoughts and feelings as dark hypotheses. Yet they were not wholly alien. Goethe had earlier flirted with melancholy, though never quite persuading himself to take it seriously. More important, his poems sometimes came close to his hero's moods—close enough to say 'there but for the grace of God . . .'. Werther's pride in the sensitive heart that makes him unique, but also drives him tyrannically back to a fatal love, is not so far from Prometheus's pride in the achievement of his 'sacredly glowing heart'; Werther's intense but unfulfilled yearnings for union with nature recall Ganymede's ecstatic transition from the beauty of a spring morning to the embracing clouds of the godhead; and Werther's horror-stricken sense of the beauty yet also destructiveness of nature echoes the Earth Spirit's sublime speech to Faust of this same period, which instead of oscillating between the two perceptions unites them and accepts them as one necessary truth.

The analogies and the neighbourhood are clear—but so is the difference. Werther's more diffuse sensibility, his aspiring and falling short, his intensity without harmony, show how close imbalance is to balance, vulnerability to strength. Werther is Goethe's pathological shadow, lacking his decisive substance: the serener set of mind, the capacity to engage the outside world, assimilate it and transform it, which are a fact of temperament and ultimately a grace of nature. The lack is fatal.

That shadow stays with Goethe. Often when he looks back at his novel, he morosely questions existence, wonders if it is not after all absurd (e.g. 3 Dec. 1812). The problem also returns in other figures and situations: can

21

man's mind and emotions come sufficiently to terms with the world to be at home there, to accept its conditions and live in it and of it? Since the question is repeatedly and honestly posed, and since Werther's was a tragic answer always to hand, it makes no sense to say that Goethe 'avoided tragedy', if by that is meant the evasion and not the successful resolution of the problems he set his characters and himself. That his work does contain such successful resolutions simply means that the 'tragic axiom' was not yet the cliché it has since become. For the time being, in the mid-seventies, Goethe takes account of the darker view but does not yield to it. He formulates it compassionately, in the fullest sense, but beyond making it poetically effective he does not revel in its exploitation. The pathos and pathology of Romantic individualism do not become his norm. It is a significant early victory.

Drama

Self-expression in lyric, delicate empathy in *Werther*—can these qualities adjust to drama, the most objective of the genres? In one peculiar form, they do so very directly. When the expressive impulse explores a myth and speaks with an assumed voice, as Prometheus or Ganymede, it is close to drama. Lengthen the text and it becomes monodrama; add a second speaking part (say, for Zeus) and it would be drama proper. In its beginnings in the 1770s, *Faust* explores the thoughts and feelings of a legendary seeker after knowledge, and through them the poet's own; it could have remained a single brooding monologue. But the lyrical impulse splits, imagines a philistine counter-voice and a devilish third role as further ways to define the central figure and his situation. This is subtly different from the way orthodox dramatists

distribute their attention among the distinct individu-
alities within a framework of action. It also has snags as
a working method. It can achieve superb character-
studies, but it gives no guarantee of coherent structures.
The expressive impulse does not plan; if it flags, the
work may be given up, or resumed later in a changed
mood and with a changed aesthetic, which will make it
an intricate compound. *Faust* is the extreme case, with
its genesis scattered over sixty years so that the final text
is the geological record of the poet's existence.

So drama begins for Goethe as a private mode, at odds
with the nature of theatre as a public forum and
untouched by the function of drama as part of a society's
understanding of itself. But in Goethe's youth German
drama and theatre were being revolutionised, and he
soon found himself in the thick of it. Since the 1750s
there had been a growing challenge to the Neo-classicism
that dominated German theatre—or rather, stood in for
an absent native theatre. Forms and themes were a
French import, catering for the tastes of the innumerable
princes and their courts who had no appetite for a
German product and no reason to believe or hope that
one was possible. Often, like Frederick the Great, they
only spoke German reluctantly (and badly). Their tastes
were no doubt largely unreflective, a passive acceptance
of what was accepted; but that made them no less
dominant. There was also a real correspondence between
the elevated style and regal characters of the Neo-
classical mode, and the elevated patrons who sustained
its prestige. Bourgeois critical minds saw the link and
conceived an alternative mode: a drama distinctively
bourgeois and German, accessible to a new audience
because it would mirror their social and national being,
rest on their values and use their language. This

initiative entailed fundamental artistic change, setting literature on the long road to social realism. 'Class' necessarily bulked larger here than 'nation'—class was a supra-national phenomenon, and its German treatment drew strength from Diderot's *drame bourgeois* in France.

Yet 'nation' remained an obsessive concern for German artists, precisely because the thing itself barely existed. The ragged entity to which they belonged, the Holy Roman Empire, inspired little feeling. The word 'fatherland' meant a home town or small state, one of the hundreds that made up the Empire. But perhaps a national drama, mysteriously appealing to all who spoke German, would somehow (if it could be created) in turn create a common feeling and help to bring a unified society and nation into being? So German themes were needed, works containing a German essence.

The demand chimed with, perhaps in part sprang from, the new 'historism': Herder's and the antiquarian Justus Möser's view that every age and culture in history was unique and had an equal right to be understood in its own terms, not simply subjected to the allegedly universal standard of judgement which a later, more 'civilised' (but really only different) society would apply. There was no longer to be a single hierarchy of historico-cultural valuations, but a plurality of historical building-blocks out of which God could be thought of as raising his edifice. And among them, as an immediate beneficiary of historist theories and perhaps their secret instigator, was German culture and its right to be its un-French self.

But where was the elusive German essence to be found? Not in the present, which the younger generation agreed was decadent, alienated from itself and dried up by a mediocre rationality. The true springs of national character and feeling must lie in the past. More than one writer tried the story of Hermann—Arminius, who defeated Varus's Roman legions in AD 9—but that was not so much tradition as regression. More recent events were needed, like those in Shakespeare's Histories; but the German past offered no such large-scale and certainly no such coherent story as Shakespeare set before English audiences, with military and moral disasters and triumphs and a hopeful outlook into the Elizabethan millennium. Shakespeare nevertheless becomes in these years the name to conjure with for the avant-garde; his authority sets the new dramatic rule—the rule of casting off rules, especially the theatrical unities which Neoclassicism claimed to find in Aristotle.

That Goethe should at this point become the German Shakespeare and write a sweepingly successful history play, *Götz von Berlichingen* (1773), seems not to fit those private expressive talents. But it was not opportunism or even versatility. In an odd way his literary character and values fitted the bill exactly, needing only to be projected on to a bigger screen. For the new idea that a culture should be free to be itself was a greater version of the expressive poet's confidence to be himself; the uniqueness of each national group was individualism writ large; and when drama emerged after a hundred and fifty years from the classroom of 'the rules' to range over time and space and freely explore the past, it was only a grander form of the poet's escape into the free world of nature. For Goethe, to emulate Shakespeare was to grasp nature on this grander scale, because Shakespeare's drama was not just a way of presenting the world, it *was* the world. Reading him, Goethe felt like a blind man given back his sight. Where continental critics like Voltaire had looked askance at Shakespeare's monstrous characters, the young Goethe cried 'Nature! Nature!

Nothing is such sheer Nature as Shakespeare's men and women!' (H 12.226). That may seem naïve—after all poetic representation, like language, and perhaps even perception itself, is not nature direct, but mediated through convention. Yet for the receptive and especially the creative imagination to work properly, the sense of direct access to an actual reality is vital. Some naïvety is needful.

But what prompted Goethe to move into the Shakespearean element himself? Once more, an identification. He chanced upon the crude autobiography of Gottfried von Berlichingen with the Iron Hand, an obscure knight of the Empire who spent much of the sixteenth century aimlessly feuding, alternately in and out of disgrace with the Emperor, taking part in crusades and getting implicated in the Peasants' Revolt of 1525. In Götz, Goethe bizarrely perceived a lost world of values. Besides his fighting prowess, Götz appears as a natural good man, an embodiment of honesty, fidelity and generosity in contrast with the cynical careerists now moving to the new centres of power. Guileless and uncomprehending, he is brought down by them and by the forces that are reshaping the Empire; law, administration, economics, and the very ethos of society are growing abstract, alien, losing touch with the old local roots. Götz is never openly defeated but is out-manœuvred, cheated. Apart from his own men, only the old Emperor keeps faith with Götz as Götz does with him; but the Emperor dies. So does Götz, much earlier in the play than in history, not killed but fading away. An age dies out with them.

The historical identification is plain and powerful. Old German virtues are preached to the eighteenth century, but are shown being defeated in the sixteenth as a pre-echo of their neglected state in Goethe's day. The past is read as a distant cause and a telling reflection of the present. Goethe himself is reflected in Götz too. Perhaps the likeness of their names struck a spark (Herder had made Goethe name-conscious by suggesting some unflattering etymologies of 'Goethe'). Certainly, when Goethe writes of his own battle with the alien abstractions that constrict the German theatre, he uses the language of dungeons and towers against which, Götz-like, he must pursue a feud (H 12.225).

At both levels, social and personal, the past is made an ally in present struggles—what Nietzsche was later to call the 'monumental use' of history. The play is none the less a colourful canvas of a past age which the modern imagination has loyally tried to see as it really was. That makes *Götz* not just a historical but a historic play: it opens up a new popular access to the past through drama and later through narrative (Sir Walter Scott's historical novels were partly inspired by *Götz*, a version of which was in 1799 his first published work). Contemporary audiences were delighted. The varied and colourful characters talking the distinctive prose of every social class were a relief after the uniform pallor of Neo-classical figures. Even more delighted were the historist thinkers and their adherents, for whom Goethe had provided the perfect object-lesson. He had set up, Herder wrote, a monument to Shakespeare from the substance of Germany's own knightly epoch.

With a publisher offering generous terms for a dozen more such plays, a public primed to receive them enthusiastically, and an ideology into which they fitted, Goethe might have gone on to give Germany an instant 'national' literature. The broad vistas of historism could paradoxically have shrunk to a narrow and intense national self-assertion, as they did in the German historians of the next century. But Goethe now steered away from that dangerous current, even while remaining true to his feeling for reality as necessarily local and concrete. The drama *Egmont*, begun next, uses the idea of unique and incommensurable cultures as a political argument against Spanish rule in the Netherlands. At the centre is Count Egmont, inescapably a political figure by his eminence, but impolitic and even irresponsible by nature, laying claim to full personal freedom of action. Yet in this he stands as an epitome of the distinctive Dutch character; and behind Alva's brutal invasion lies an attempt to force the Dutch into an alien mould, to destroy their individuality by denying them the ancient laws and customs from which it is inseparable. This is historist thinking again, but when used to commemorate the struggles of a different nation it regains its true all-embracing cosmopolitan nature. However different its tactics—defending a set of ancient particular freedoms for one ethnic group, rather than demanding a single new abstract Liberty for all Mankind—it becomes a useful ally of the more abstract Enlightenment case against tyranny. *Egmont* shows the limitations but also the power of a politics of individualism—something which has become familiar since, in the claims of ethnic groups large and small.

2 Order

Weimar

By 1775 the author of *Götz* and *Werther* (the poems were known, if at all, only to friends) was a national celebrity, something of an *enfant terrible*, and the central figure of a group of 'wild' young writers whom history has called, after one of their plays, the 'Sturm und Drang' (Storm and Stress) group. Only a ruler himself as young and wild as Carl August could have thought of putting such a man to practical work in his domains. Their meeting was a fortunate chance. Goethe was cramped by Frankfurt and legal practice. The duchy of Weimar gave him scope for activity, small though it was—in fact, precisely by being so small it offered direct returns for the effort of running and trying to reform its administration. Despite the raised eyebrows of aristocrats and career administrators, 'Dr Goethe' was given a place on the governing Conseil, he took over mines, roads, and the (toy) army; later he was brought in to sort out a tangled Exchequer. These concerns absorbed the greater part of his energies for the next ten years, and his official papers make a substantial volume. The literary celebrity vanished from sight. It was as if Byron, after publishing *Childe Harold*, had joined the Civil Service.

There was a clear short-term loss. Though Goethe still wrote, he had little chance of carrying through substantial projects. The effects of an unmethodical, inspirational approach to writing were compounded by lack of time, and this decade saw only one major work completed—the drama *Iphigenie*—even that not in its final verse form. Lyrical poems depend less on leisure, especially when the

poet has responses as prompt as Goethe's, but there was
loss here too. The early vigour and rhythmic drive
slacken, the colour pales, the immediate rapport with
the natural world weakens as a new reflectiveness sets
in. Where nature is still the subject, the poet casts about
uncertainly for the scent. More frequently now he treats
man's place and fate abstractly and allegorically, a mode
which is as far from the quick of inspiration as a lyrical
poet can get. The result is lucid, measured reflections
which would grace any other *œuvre* but are an anti-
climax after Goethe's magnificent opening. His exuberant emotions had been calmed and his spiritual world
narrowed in scope by his relationship with an insistently
platonic married lady of the court, Charlotte von Stein.
This decorous affair doubtless brought him comfort: he
celebrates her soothing, restoring influence in eloquent
lines that suggest (to her shock) that she was his sister or
wife in an earlier incarnation. But whatever the private
benefit, the poetic impetus is curbed. It no longer moves
out into a zestfully apprehended world, but largely loses
itself in introspective musings.

With the little that Goethe did write staying un-
published, it must have seemed to the public that a
literary comet had burned itself out, as the other young
men of the 'Storm and Stress' group had done. In fact for
Goethe these years were a preparation for a much longer
course. His duties gave him contacts with the real world
of a more complex kind than those which he had made as
a poet exploring and responding to nature. Overseeing
lowly people and the welfare of communities offered
sober perspectives on existence. Some individual contacts were valuable too. The Duke was an education in
himself, forcing responsibility on his adviser: the half-
blind led the blind and gained sight in the process. The

friendship lasted for life, despite Goethe's early recognition that the ducal court was a cruel imposition:

> I see the peasant winning bare necessities from the earth, which would be a comfortable livelihood if he only sweated for himself . . . but when the aphids on the rose-stems are nice and fat and green, along come the ants and suck the filtered sap from their bodies. So it goes on, and we have reached the point where more is always consumed in one day at the top than can be brought together at the bottom. (17 April 1782)

His attitude to the court and to princely absolutism generally was at best ironic in the manner (he once says) of Shakespeare's Jaques. His comments later on the German princes' invasion of France in 1792 ('one of the most wretched undertakings in the annals of the world') are those of an essential bystander. He is with them but not of them. All these things were contributions to 'balance' and 'experience', vital to a dramatist and novelist, as he realised. His later summary of this decade was: 'Poetic talent in conflict with reality, which . . . it is compelled to assimilate, to its higher advantage' (E 10 Feb. 1829).

But much the most important new thing in this decade was Goethe's interest in science. Outwardly it arose from his duties—inspecting the ducal forests provoked his interest in botany, patrolling Thuringia aroused his curiosity about its rock-formations; essentially, it was a continuation of the poet's encounter with the physical world, a deepening and generalising of his first intuitions. Yet, logical though that continuation is, it remains astounding. What other poet has ever matched supreme evocations of the natural world with fifty years of devoted collecting, experimenting and theorising, given new directions to science and produced a coherent body of scientific thought which still challenges attention?

The growing enthusiasm for science combined with practical work to push Goethe's writing into a very subordinate place. He had by now a handful of works unfinished on his desk and his conscience, a set of questions demanding answers. He was increasingly oppressed by the pettiness of the court, the drudgery of administration, the tensions of his private life, and some kind of psychosomatic ills to which he later cryptically refers (19 and 25 Jan. 1788). So on the morning of 3 September 1786, clandestinely at 3 a.m. ('they wouldn't have let me go otherwise') he cut loose and left for Italy. He stayed away nearly two years.

Italy

This new escape into the 'free world' reasserts Goethe's own rights after a decade spent accommodating himself to the wishes and needs of others—a demanding but ungiving mistress, a tedious court circle, a ramshackle principality. Self-realisation becomes the overriding aim, what earlier he had called 'the desire to raise the pyramid of my existence, whose base is given and founded for me, as high in the air as possible' (20 Sept. 1780). To do this he must now 'banish what I have so long considered my duty, and recognise that a man has to take the good things that come his way as a fortunate find, not looking to left or right, much less bothering with the happiness or unhappiness of a larger whole' (20 Jan. 1787). When he writes this, he is already in Rome.

Going to Italy was in a sense an unoriginal way to assert himself. The cultural riches Italy offered were a post-Renaissance commonplace. Goethe was following Dürer, Montaigne and many others; Winckelmann had found the inspiration for his art-history there and German painters were already colonising Rome (Goethe joined their community). Yet his desire was strangely sharp and personal. It had long been a dream to follow in the footsteps of his father, whose memories and souvenirs of Italy were part of the landscape of Goethe's childhood. More than once it had been foiled on the edge of accomplishment, and he became increasingly obsessed with this particular release from his Weimar problems (in the mid-eighties he was pathologically sensitive to any reminder of Italy, even a Classical text). The diary of his eight-week journey to Rome is full of yearning for a destination which is also a destiny. He hastens past places of interest 'to carry through the one idea which has almost grown too old in my soul' (D 5 Sept. 1786). There are superstitious fears that he may be struck dead by the angel of the Lord before arriving. And then Rome, relief and exhilaration: 'Only now do I begin to live, and give reverent thanks to my guardian spirit' (D 29 Oct. 1786).

This almost mystical expectancy helps explain Goethe's experience of Italy as both confirmation and transformation, foreseen fulfilment and exciting novelty. The first letter from Rome to Weimar friends says:

> I have had no wholly new ideas, found nothing wholly strange, but the old ideas have become so definite, so live, so coherent, that they may count as new. When Pygmalion's Eliza, whom he had shaped exactly to his wishes and given as much truth and reality to as an artist can, came towards him saying Now I really *am*, how different was the living woman from the hewn stone! (1 Nov. 1786)

The image aptly states the difference between expec-

33

tation and realisation. It also implies that Goethe's enthusiasm was not an escape from realities into fantasy: the sculptor's labours in the myth are matched by Goethe's ten years of maturing, attending to hard facts, learning to observe and record judiciously, going beyond practical tasks to scientific knowledge and speculation. All of which only needed a transforming touch—a mellower climate, literally and metaphorically—to bring it together into a satisfying unity. Italy, of all places, offered perfect objects to match every one of Goethe's interests and developed sensibilities: beauty of landscape and a richer vegetation, great buildings (especially those of Palladio) and noble ruins, eloquent remains of ancient life and art, some great modern painting (especially Michelangelo and Raphael) and sites rich in association with the literature and history of antiquity—all of them enhanced by the clear Mediterranean light which was itself a revelation to the 'barbarian' visitor ('We Cimmerians barely know what a *day* is, in our eternal mist and gloom'—D 17 Sept. 1786). Before he even reaches Italy, the travel-diary shows his senses coming alive and drinking in perceptions, rejoicing in the loss of constriction. Before he reaches Rome he is gratefully registering the 'revolution' taking place within him. But the full range of his Roman experience makes him feel positively reborn. The mind that once responded with such freshness to a nature no other poet had captured responds now to a culture all Europe had long taken for granted. It is a personal renascence.

What does he do in Rome? Above all, he *sees*. He goes about filling and over-filling his mind with impressions, pauses for a while to assimilate them, then begins all over again. But it is the quality of seeing rather than the quantity that matters. He tunes his whole organism to see clearly and (in his word) 'purely'. 'I am living frugally and keeping calm so that objects do not find a heightened mind, but themselves heighten it' (D 24 Sept. 1786). In fact, 'heightening' as conventionally meant is irrelevant to true seeing: 'If you . . . were to see the objects here, you would have the greatest of pleasure, for in the end all the heightening and embellishing power of the imagination cannot conceive that which is True.' The streets of Rome are paved with the gold of visual truth: 'Anyone who looks about him seriously here and has eyes to see, must become *solid,* he must get a conception of solidity such as was never so vivid to him before. To me at least it is as if I had never appraised the things of this world aright as I now do here' (7 Nov. 1786). This strange usage of 'becoming solid' (*solid werden*) recurs three days later as 'an inner solidity with which the mind so to speak is stamped'. It is as if the revelation of exact seeing gives the observer himself the unshakeable rightness of a Classical building; the mass and harmony which the eye sees impose themselves on the mind and make it in the most direct sense 'objective'.

The process is not a single absolute change at a stroke, but could be continued. Three months in Rome have transformed his way of seeing, so what would years do? And how much would be left to do even then? It would take 'a lifetime of activity and practice to bring our knowledge to the highest point of purity. And yet only this security and certainty of taking things for what they really are . . . would be the supreme enjoyment that we should strive after in art, nature and life itself' (23 Dec. 1786). The process is in part an ethical one; it involves giving up all pretension, prejudice and self-will, and waiting humbly for reality to flood in through the eye —something far more radical than the course in

35

connoisseurship and drawing-technique Goethe was outwardly engaged in as he did the sights and took lessons
from the painter Tischbein. Anyone can take in Rome,
see the villas, museums and ruins, indulge in feeling and
reflection: 'But when it is a matter of seeing things for
their own sake, going to the marrow of the arts, judging
what has been shaped not in terms of its effect on us but
according to its own inner value—then one feels how
hard the task is' (23 Dec. 1786). This is no occupation for
dilettantes but a serious study, akin to the study of
nature. Increasingly Goethe links the two. His scientific
knowledge of nature helps his understanding of ancient
art because the ancients followed nature faithfully. He
has 'fortunately found a way to combine art with my
way of thinking about nature, so that both have become
doubly dear to me' (3 Oct. 1787). So when the 'ceremonies
and operas' of the Church fail to impress him, his two
loves serve equally as a contrast: 'A natural phenomenon, a work of art like the much revered Juno are the
only things that make a deep and permanent effect' (6
Jan. 1787). (He has 'colossal' heads of Juno and Jupiter in
his lodgings, just as in Weimar he had an elephant's
skull in his room when working on anatomy.)

Goethe's linking of art and nature is neither rhetorical
nor just a matter of the chance coincidence of his
interests. As he penetrates further into each area, the
laws underlying them appear more and more similar.
Both have an inner necessity. Nature's 'consistent truth'
is matched by the greatest works of man: in Raphael and
Palladio there is 'not an ounce of arbitrariness, they knew
the limits and laws of their art in the highest degree and
moved within them with ease' (D 19 Oct. 1786). A small
temple of Minerva near Assisi he calls 'so natural' (the
word must be given its full weight) 'and so great in its

naturalness' (D 26 Oct. 1786). He gets the same intense satisfaction from a living thing, a small crab seen at Venice: 'How precisely fitted to its condition, how true! how *full of being!' (wie wahr! wie* seiend!—D 9 Oct. 1786). He sees now what is wrong with the trivial products of art he has left behind in Germany: 'Whatever has no true inner existence has no life and cannot be made to live and cannot be great or become great' (D 27 Oct. 1786). That notion of an inner life-principle working its way out from a central germination to a developed form is for Goethe applicable to works of art and natural phenomena equally and literally. His recurrent phrase for such development, 'outwards from within' (*von innen heraus*), leaps from one context to the other, always signifying a harmonious obedience to appropriate laws which is open to sympathetic perception by the student of art or science. It is the principle of Palladio's greatness, it is the thread which the artist studying anatomy must pursue, and it is the force at work in Goethe's own life amid the welter of new experience: 'so much is thrusting in on me that I can't fend it off, my existence is growing like a snowball, and it's as if my mind can't grasp or stand it all, and yet everything is developing outwards from within, and I cannot live without that' (D 27 Sept. 1786).

The implication is plain. Nature, existence as part of nature, and human art as a natural product of man are all shaped and controlled by the same fundamental forces and laws. A grand monism is within reach, an all-embracing theory of harmonious growth which is simple in its general outline but allows infinite refinement and complexity in its detail. It also allows man a comforting awareness of belonging to the natural order, something Goethe's early poetry had intuitively grasped. The act of coming to Italy is itself the operation of a force of nature within him, an unfolding of his specific individual being. His response to all of this is a reverence which gives new sense to old concepts: of those 'high works of art' which are also 'the highest works of nature', Goethe can say '*There* is necessity, *there* is God' (H 11.395).

If that is indeed where necessity and God are, it follows they cannot be somewhere quite different—in the theatrical rituals by which the Church keeps 'a lie' alive in the popular mind, or in the 'repellent stupid subjects' which have so long been the 'scourge' of painters (D 8 Oct. 1786). Goethe's revulsion from crucifixions and martyrdoms is matched by his sympathy for the artist who was forced to work against the grain of his art: 'Not one subject in ten fit to be painted, and when there was one, he wasn't allowed to take it from the right side.' Renaissance religious pictures—a Tintoretto or Guido Reni—are thus 'everything a painter could do and everything senseless that could be demanded of him' (D 19 Oct. 1786). Only in occasional figures and details could he show what he might have done if given a free hand.

Goethe's objections are not just emotional, but technical. His understanding of what visual art is or should be fuses with his conviction of man's right relation to the world that art portrays. When he complains that Christian art has 'never a present interest, always some fantastical expectation', he is rejecting on aesthetic grounds pictures whose meaning lies outside themselves, even as Christian values lie ultimately outside the world. Crucifixion and martyrdom loom so large only because they promise to carry men there, to paradise. They are not in themselves pictorially engaging objects. What would a culture that knew nothing of Christian doctrines make of this sad harvest? Visual phenomena have been misused, even in a sense by-passed; they have become (as

Walter Pater put it) 'the sensuous expression of conceptions which unreservedly discredit the world of sense'.
For Goethe, painting should represent objects for their
own sake as part of earthly life, deserving to be seen,
recorded and celebrated in their own right. (Accordingly
he had no aversion to the Virgin, as a potentially natural
symbol.)

Goethe is here being consistent and radical where
earlier admirers of antiquity often kept their admiration
from getting at their orthodox Christian beliefs. His
thought combines a pagan attachment to the things of
this earth with the fundamental insights of Lessing's
aesthetic essay *Laokoon* of 1766. This argued that visual
art was limited by its medium to the representation of
bodies coexistent in space and was denatured if used to
tell a story (only literature could properly handle events
consecutive in time) or to point an allegorical meaning
that lay outside the physical reality rendered by paint or
carved stone.

How specifically pagan Goethe's inspiration is, and
how far the differing practice of Christian and pagan art
reflects for him an ideological contrast, is plain from his
response to an ancient sarcophagus with its characteristic
ethos in the face of death:

A father appears to be taking leave of his family on his
death-bed . . . The presence of the stones moved me
greatly, so that I could not hold back tears. Here is no
man in armour on his knees, waiting for a joyful
resurrection, the artist has consistently put before us
with such skill as he had only the simple present of
these human beings and has thereby extended their
existence and given it permanence. They do not put
their hands together and look up at the sky, rather they
are what they were, they stand together, they feel for

39

one another, they love each other, and that is expressed in the stone, often with a certain lack of technique, most sweetly. (D 16 Sept. 1786)

Far from projecting thought and feeling beyond the bounds of earth and art, the sculptor has drawn death as far as possible into life. 'The breeze that blows from the graves of the ancients comes laden with fragrance, as from a mound of roses.' The 'very earthly' young man with his 'truth of the five senses' and his contentment to 'dwell in himself' has found his spiritual home in a culture which even in death can celebrate life.

Love

In Rome Goethe went beyond sight to achieve vision, a sober vision with no prophetic pretensions, but a kind of revelation none the less. In so far as objectivity is humanly possible (Goethe was never much afflicted with epistemological scepticism) he believed he had attained it. The mere belief was enough, in a man of his talents, to inspire great things. But when he bore his revelation back to Weimar, no one was interested. His absence and obvious pleasure in Italy had been resented; his return was not fêted. He had never been an assiduous courtier, and this coolness was hardly encouraging. The duchy and its minds seemed narrower than ever to a man whose horizons in space and time had broadened. Goethe withdrew into his private world.

What he did there disconcerted Weimar. He took a mistress, a girl of modest social background, and in due course again made his pleasure known, in a unique cycle of poems that are his first truly Classical work. The *Römische Elegien* (Roman Elegies) describe a happy sexual love such as is scarcely found elsewhere in Western lyric. There is none of the despairing desire, cruel loss, failed fulfilment, hearts broken by circumstance, worship from afar, spiritual sublimation or madonna-mystery—in short, none of the normal (!) stimulants of the genre. Goethe speaks of love freely given, promptly accepted and willingly reciprocated. He is too much concerned with love to isolate sex, but too delighted by sex not to celebrate it enthusiastically and tenderly. Defiantly too, here and there, since he cannot fail to see that uninhibited loving in an inhibited society is a provocation. But he wastes little time on that contrast, which is fortunate, since the proclaiming of sex as the way to human balance can easily sound unbalanced in its shrillness (D. H. Lawrence), the remedy itself seem part of the ailment. Goethe's mood is altogether more relaxed and secure.

Outwardly he emulates the Latin love-poets, Propertius, Tibullus, Catullus; he uses their elegiac couplets (hexameter-plus-pentameter) and he invokes their authority for his way of loving and writing. Yet in neither is he really like them. Goethe's emotional tone is warmer, and, for all his active love-making, gentler; love is mutuality, not conflict. Where Propertius's Cynthia is sophisticated and bitchy, Goethe's Faustine is simple and sincere, even domestic—she rekindles the real fire as well as his from the ashes of the morning after. Nevertheless, for Goethe the sense of tradition is a powerful force. He feels he has returned to an older, better way of life which ancient literature has kept open—for if a cultural value is real, not merely something that has conventional prestige, it must be possible to relive it as it once was:

When those happy men lived, 'antiquity' was a *new* thing!
Live life happily—so history will live on in you!

> (War das Antike doch neu, da jene Glücklichen lebten!
> Lebe glücklich, und so lebe die Vorzeit in dir!)
>
> (Elegy XIII)

Antiquity was simply more human—'humaniora' is taken with a disarming literalness.

Rome herself, as well as her poets, is part of the cycle. The grand historical setting intensifies the excitement of love, but also balances it. The lover's impatience for nightfall is allayed by the sights of the city and thoughts of its great past: typically of a truly Classical poetry, the range of emotions is not broadened but narrowed, fruitlessly ethereal yearning is excluded by the substantial content given to the hours of waiting. The two terms of Goethe's original title—'Erotica romana'—are equal partners. There is a balance between diverse yet related interests, as there is again in the not merely playful perception that love-making and the study of statues have each intensified his enjoyment and understanding of the other, transposed the sense-skills at work, giving him 'Eyes that can feel like a hand, hands that can see like an eye' ('Sehe mit fühlendem Aug', fühle mit sehender Hand'—Elegy V). And there is balance too in the form, which flows equably on, declining to turn sexual experience into the pointed formulations of wit: how different it would all sound, said Goethe on looking back, in the rhymed stanzas that Byron used for his *Don Juan* (E 25 Jan. 1824).

So did it all really happen in Rome? W. H. Auden thought that the post-Italian portraits showed the 'self-assured face of a man who has known sexual satisfaction', compared with the visible 'neurasthenia' of earlier pictures. Goethe's image of Pygmalion's statue coming alive may seem suggestive. But to read his Italian expectancy as displaced sexual appetite would be too simple; and his later letters from Italy make it plain that there were too many obstacles, social and hygienic, to sexual indulgence there (e.g. 29 Dec. 1787). What really matters is that at some time in these years, through Christiane Vulpius in Weimar if not sooner, Goethe experienced love as something real, natural, and needing to be no more than that. Like his observation of nature and art in Italy, it needed no 'heightening' by fantasy. The result is a poetry for adults, not because it is prurient but because it is not. That, paradoxically, is what shocked contemporaries: Goethe was clearly not playing the accepted eighteenth-century game of literary titillation, he was talking about realities. That had radical implications for poetry and for life.

The connection of love with art and nature is not just a formal analogy. By stepping outside the social and moral conventions of his day into a freer pagan ethos, Goethe made himself part of the natural order he had studied as a scientist and as a devotee of art. No wonder the woman in the *Elegies* is called Faustine, for she is part of the answer to a Faustian quest for the reality of the world, a last perfecting touch. Love, nature and art, spontaneity and culture, present and past, have joined in a deeply satisfying nexus. Goethe is a whole man within a harmonious totality. At the centre of it, his relationship with Christiane grows like a natural organism, bud, blossom and fruit. That is the closing thought of another great elegy addressed to her (H 1.201). It is a poem far removed from the usual area of love-lyrics: its subject is the metamorphosis of plants.

Science

In his opening monologue, Goethe's Faust thirsts for a vision of the world's inmost cohesive forces and spurns

43

the arid academic word-mongering of his life so far. The same impulse informs Goethe's science. He rejects from the start all rigid classifications and the authority of labels. Against the 'dividing and counting' of plants and their parts on which Linnaean botany rested, he revels in the variations which blur the borders between species. He is more interested in relating than dividing, and aspires to supplement Linnaeus's *Genera plantarum* with a *Harmonia plantarum*. Similarly he collects rock samples that lie between known types and defy geological system. System is a human importation, a rigid frame imposed on a fluid reality. 'Nature has no system, it has—it is—life and continuity from an unknown centre to a limit we cannot discern' (H 13.35).

The pursuit of intermediate specimens recalls the ancient notion, probably known to Goethe in its most recent Leibnizian form, of a 'Great Chain of Being', in which the kindness of a God who would not deny life to any possible creature entailed ever more finely differentiated forms to fill ever smaller gaps. But for Goethe what matters is not the forms themselves produced by discrete divine acts, but (so to speak) the process running through them. Stasis lurches into movement, 'intermediate' becomes 'transitional' and a new approach to phenomena begins: morphology, the science of developing forms. Nature becomes a realm of 'mobile order' (H 1.203).

It was also for Goethe one of ultimate unity. This too was not a new idea, but it could still be controversial. For theologians and some scientists of the day, man was not just the peak of creation but an isolated peak, discontinuous in his basic structures from the higher animals. Sure enough, man alone seemed to lack the intermaxillary bone—Q.E.D. But Goethe (and others about the same time, like the Frenchman Viq d'Azyr—priority is not at issue) found it there after all, in vestigial form. This repaired nature's continuum. What for the orthodox meant degrading man, in Goethe's eyes completed him, confirming his place in the natural order. That in itself not very significant bone was the 'keystone of man'. Analogy and homology continued to be central to Goethe's scientific thought.

Plainly, his science was not just an ancillary to his practical duties, though they were its occasion. It elaborated his poet's intuition of the coherence and value of earthly things. Enthused by scientific study, he urges Charlotte von Stein to become a 'friend of the earth' (9 Sept. 1780). Sometimes his enthusiasm rises to near-poetry:

> What most delights me now is the plant world that pursues me; and that really is the way a thing becomes your own. Everything forces itself upon me, I no longer reflect on it, it all comes to meet me and the immense realm is simplifying itself in my mind so that soon I shall be able to read off the most difficult problem straight away. If only I could convey the eye for it and the pleasure of it to somebody, but it isn't possible. And it is no dream, no fantasy; it is a perception of the essential form with which so to speak nature is constantly playing, and bringing forth as it plays the manifold forms of life. If I had time in the short space of one lifetime, I believe I could extend it to all the realms of nature—to her whole realm. (9 July 1786)

These intuitions also now had a kind of philosophical backing. In the mid-1780s controversy again flared over the atheism of Spinoza. Goethe re-read him, felt a deep affinity with his view of nature, and saw in the *Ethics* a programme for scientific research, of a kind that embraced love and reverence for the things investigated. Spinoza had written: 'The more we understand individual things, the more we understand God'—an immanent God, that is, accessible (so Goethe read Spinoza) to direct seeing, not just unguaranteed faith. This account of 'intuitive knowledge' (*scientia intuitiva*), moving from the 'formal essence' of the divine attributes to the 'formal essence' of things, gave Goethe 'the courage to devote my whole life to the contemplation of things' (5 May 1786).

Revealingly, he has transposed the dry scholastic term 'formal essence' (*essentia formalis*) into his own typically dynamic 'essential form' (*wesentliche Form*). Revealingly in a different way, the direct perception of an essential form is linked with the pressure of time on the individual observer. Francis Bacon had proposed a 'boundless empiricism' in which all observations were equal—and innumerable. So 'before one can get to the stage of induction, even such induction as Bacon advocates, before one can get to the stage of simplification and conclusion, life goes by and one's powers are exhausted' (H 14.91). There must surely be a way to grasp many instances in one representative case, an archetype or 'primal phenomenon' (*Urphänomen*) beyond which man then need not go. The limits set for human existence help to dictate the quality scientific truth shall have.

These pressures and aspirations shape Goethe's scientific thinking and method. He insists on the study of individual phenomena, and is to that extent an empiricist. But he is always looking beyond analysis to synthesis; general and particular are held in balance and 'seen' together; the parts of the book of nature are read in the light of the whole, 'otherwise every separate thing is only a dead letter' (17 Nov. 1784). The—in some sense—divine ground and wholeness of the world are presupposed, and to that extent Goethe is a metaphysician.

A typical product of this dual impulse is the notion of the 'primal plant' (*Urpflanze*), the model of plant growth he was groping towards before Italy. It developed rapidly in the southern climate and in response to the southern flora—'Many things that at home I only suspected and sought for with the microscope, I can see here with my own eyes as a certainty beyond doubt' (18 Aug. 1787)—and it finally burst on his mind in a public garden in Palermo. For him it was the form all plants had developed from, it was visible to his eye in the configuration of every one of them, and it was what allowed him to recognise a plant as such. These very disparate functions, pointing back to the preoccupations of Plato as much as they pointed onward to those of Darwin, are hardly to be carried out by a single entity. If Goethe could 'see' his primal plant in every specimen, as he insisted when Schiller called it 'not an experience but an idea' (H 10.540 f.), then that was only because what the eye sees is in large measure what the mind is expecting and seeking. If one primal plant was the original for all plants, then it was only in the sense that an initial model could be conceived for a set of plant organs, each with infinite possibilities, to be combined in infinite permutations (something the poem 'Die Metamorphose der Pflanzen' (Metamorphosis of Plants) conveys lucidly and beautifully). As for recognising a plant as a plant, nothing more novel was needed for that than a concept. Some epistemological confusion is plain; but so is the symbolic cohesiveness of Goethe's approach to things.

The same quality is present in his idea that the most

fundamental plant organ was the leaf, all the others being modifications, caused by a gradual refinement of the sap as it moves outwards; or in the idea which applies a similar method to anatomy and explains the mammalian skull as a modification of the vertebrae; or again in the idea of compensation in animal development which ensures that hypertrophy of one organ (e.g. horns) will be balanced by a reduction in another (e.g. teeth), as if the animal were a quantum of potential growth contained in a flexible ring. Each is a brilliant *aperçu*, a perception of formal possibilities often reached in a sudden quasi-poetic inspiration. Not without long preparatory work—Goethe was no dilettante, he made extensive and minute observations and he was committed to experiment as the means of rectifying the understanding so as to achieve a 'pure' vision of phenomena (H 13.25). But essentially he was operating with the eye of the imagination.

This approach is of course not peculiar to poets. Good scientists develop a quasi-aesthetic intuitive 'feel' in respect of the phenomena they study, which runs ahead of and then has to be checked by analytical procedures. Leaps of the imagination can carry a science forward at a critical juncture in its history. The life-sciences were at such a juncture in Goethe's day, and his morphological method was the right and fruitful direction of development, even if many of his results are now known to have been wrong in detail. True, his thinking is not in all points as modern as it may seem: he conceives development as springing from inherent principles of growth, with environment playing only a subsidiary role, and is thus nearer to St Augustine's 'seminal reasons' than to Darwinian evolution. But he has left pre-scientific teleology behind and helped to open the free play of nature to those later interpretations that will go beyond the forms to the controlling forces of selection and gene, and bear out even more dramatically his view that species are only phases in an endless flux. Goethe's place in the history of biology is safe.

But where perceptions of form and transformation were not central, Goethe could be at cross-purposes with science. This was most disastrously the case in his long, bitter polemic against Newton's theory of light and colour. It was not just that Goethe misunderstood Newton to be saying 'that clear, pure, unsullied light is composed of dark lights'; or that he reviled Newton for bad faith, for 'anticipating' truth, imposing an *a priori* view and then using all his ingenuity to defend it; or that he accused the scientific community of being cowed into conformity by Newton's prestige. (He had some grounds for this suspicion in so far as his own earlier theories had been dismissed largely because he was not one of the guild.) It was rather that he pressed his attack further, against scientific analysis itself because it went beyond what could be seen, dissolving light and colour into the abstractions of physics, and thereby destroying the very phenomenon itself as the human observer knows it.

This was the weakness of Goethe's strength: the commitment to wholeness that carried him beyond Linnaeus makes him fall short of Newton. The frustration of battling against an established but 'mistaken' view drives him to extremes. He rejects the use of mathematics (which he elsewhere respects), shuns deliberately devised experiments (which he elsewhere practises), discourages the use of instruments (which he elsewhere allows), and declares the 'primal phenomena' of light and dark, which in his theory make up colour, to be limiting cases that man not only need not but must not go beyond. By all these means, he seems to be setting bounds to scientific probing. 'The uninvestigable' which he elsewhere speaks of as a necessary residue when science has pressed as far as it can, here becomes a sanctum which science may not enter.

This has made him in recent times a much-invoked ally of writers with doubts about or animus towards modern science. His insistence on self-limitation is celebrated as a wisdom to which man should return. The key concept is 'wholeness': the qualitative wholeness of the phenomenon, which science ought not to dissolve into quantitative abstraction; the corresponding wholeness of the human student, from which a neutral, 'abstract' scientific observer ought not to be separated out; and the wholeness of science itself, which ought to be kept actively in view as a condition of every monographic investigation.

This last point excepted, the 'wisdom' is surely untenable, a caricature of Goethe's best tendencies. It shows him refusing to follow the logic of his own empiricism; for if observation of phenomena is to be progressively 'purified', then qualitative nuances of form must eventually become quantities to be measured with micro-precision. By its whole history and rationale, science pursues the nature of things to levels beyond the power of the 'whole' human being to perceive with unaided bodily organs. To resist this progression—to insist that man himself is 'the perfect and most precise apparatus for physics that there can be' (H 12.458)—is to make science not just anthropocentric but anthropomorphic. Science inevitably travels away from life and the world as sense and common sense and even artistic vision know them, to find at the end of the journey (in

Werner Heisenberg's words) 'no longer life and no longer world, but instead understanding and clarity with regard to the ideas in accordance with which the world is constructed'.

Science is also irretrievably a partial activity of the human being, one unit in the division of intellectual labour. Restoring 'wholeness' after this as after any other partial activity is a task which must lie outside the activity itself, as Schiller demonstrated in his *Aesthetic Letters* of 1795 (*Briefe über die ästhetische Erziehung des Menschen*), which encompass the whole problem. To try to restore human wholeness *within* the partial activity is a confusion of categories. That the contribution of science to man's total achievement and needs should be integrated as only one element in the broader range of his interests is another matter, a more serious necessity from which 'Goethean' attacks on modern science can only distract attention and effort. But keeping science in its place intellectually and socially, as only one view of several that arise from man's nature and must all have a voice, does not at all mean denying science its right to specialisation, abstraction and precision within its own sphere.

It is easy enough, especially for disgruntled non-scientists, to assail modern science. But it is also perilous to reject scientific rigour in the name of private qualitative intuitions which claim descent from Goethe and whose status then rests, in a reversal of the argument by which Goethe's contemporaries dismissed his theories, on his prestige as a poet. Perilous, because since the seventeenth century science has been not just a technique for investigating and manipulating nature, but also an intellectual tradition and paradigm of argument and verification with implications far beyond its own sphere. Attacks on scientific objectivity and rationality have often been accompanied, not coincidentally, by attacks on other basic values. What then guarantees the quality of the 'qualitative' alternative? One need only recall that in 1933 the poet and Nazi fellow-traveller Gottfried Benn, who had pretensions to scientific knowledge, publicly glorified Goethe's science as 'the first rejection of European intellectualism' and of the Newtonian 'objective world' in favour of an 'existential and transcendent world' which alone mattered. Such a renewal was allegedly going forward at that time in Germany—that is, the wholesale plunge into irrationalism which was totally to destroy German intellectual standards and much more.

Goethe the scientist needs rescuing from the admirers who cultivate his extremes and make him out to be virtually an obscurantist. In fact, nobody who founded a far-reaching new approach in one area of science can properly be presented as retrogressive. A possibility for anyone not in principle opposed to modern scientific method, and therefore not in need of a stalking-horse, would be simply to conclude that Goethe was good at some sciences and bad at others. Yet that would be an ungenerous judgement in the larger context of his life's work and the even larger context of the relation of poets generally to the world as studied by science. For Goethe was more fully engaged with the physical world as an object of enquiry, nearer to a detailed grasp of its workings, and more active in furthering and spreading scientific knowledge than any other major poet has been, except perhaps the Lucretius he admired. All his later poetry takes account implicitly of that large extra-poetic reality; it is enriched by the mood—far more often harmonious than polemical—that grows from his understanding of the world as a place where man's body, mind and emotions can be at home. At home, that is, not just in cosy inertia, but as active participants in the constant activity of the world. This is perhaps the deepest of Goethe's intuitions, that man is movement within movement; and it is in harmony with some of the fundamental discoveries of science since his time. For all his attachment to the human scale and his dislike of abstraction, he would surely have been fascinated by particle physics, where extreme abstraction from 'reality' as we know it visualises minute worlds within worlds and translates inert matter into movement, true to Goethe's own dictum: '"State" is a foolish word, because nothing stands still and everything is in motion' (23 Nov. 1812).

3 Classicism

The fruit of these experiments and influences was a phase of Classical writing—outwardly Classical in its forms and themes, but (more importantly) Classical in essence too, because Goethe's individualism had freely found its own balance, sense of order, and norms. This was not a recantation of his early individualism—it grew naturally and unforcedly out of it. But there is still a pleasing paradox. 'Classicism' always implies harmony and control and a restraining or supportive order, but these things are usually derived from outside, often from a stable society whose ethos is reflected—may demand to be reflected—in art. Goethe has no such community to give him support or make demands; there was in his time virtually no 'German society', at all events none coherent enough for that cultural role. In its absence, he created one man's order; a formal culture grounded in natural impulse; a personal and individual—if we want to push paradox to the extreme, a Romantic—Classicism.

The paradox of his Classicism can be no objection to its substance. Goethe's vision of existence and of man is as rich and fine as anything earlier Classicisms can show. This was in itself, even apart from the works it generated, a historic achievement. Over the next decades, Romanticism was to unmake the old European world of beliefs, rules and conventions in the name of that same individualism which was Goethe's strength. But it could not remake the world anew in a single coherent image. Goethe, at the very outset of the upheaval, did precisely that. This last European Classicism is thus anything but a late derivative or epigonistic sideshow to the main cultural action of the age, it is an authentic creation and a measure of what individual power and versatility can achieve.

Goethe's isolation, fortunately for him, did not remain total. Something of what society did not give was provided by another isolated individual, Friedrich Schiller. It was a stroke of luck that a literary partner should appear just when most wanted. But Schiller was also a fine critic, of the rare kind that can perceive the largest historical and cultural issues as precisely as the quality of one line of verse. His remarkable first act of friendship was to write Goethe a letter explaining him to himself—the growth of his mind, his place in cultural history, his role in the German present. It was the seed of a brilliant essay, *On naïve and sentimental Poetry (Über naive und sentimentalische Dichtung)*, written soon after. The Goethe who had trusted implicitly in nature and felt an instinctive affinity with the ancients now learned why. His career from early poetry to mature vision fell into place in a theory which saw nature not as the fundamental antithesis of culture, but as its first and normative phase. Much as Rousseau had imagined a state of nature as man's pre-social origin, Schiller presented intuitive oneness with nature as the basis of man's earliest perception and artistic rendering of the world. Such 'naïve' oneness was a rare survival in modern times. All European vernacular literature suffered from its loss, and could only yearn and aspire 'sentimentally' to regain it or some higher analogue of it. Whatever the historical reasons for this sequence—the Christian conscience which complicated man's instinctual world with radical inner conflicts, or the philosophical 'Fall' of man into a hindering self-consciousness—

reflectiveness was the necessary burden (in both senses) of modern writing. True, reflectiveness offered infinite literary potential. But for that very reason it placed the closed perfection of ancient works beyond the modern reach. There had been a few happy exceptions to this historical fate: Shakespeare, Cervantes, Molière. And now, as a precious live specimen round whom Schiller's thought could take shape, there was Goethe. In him Schiller saw the unbroken link with nature, the 'pure' objective gaze not clouded by inner division, the instinctive spontaneity of the creative act, the perfection of finite forms—in short, the 'naïve' poet. Drawing these threads together, Schiller's theory 'placed' Goethe in perspectives even more grandiose than he had been aware of. It was a final integration of his individualism into a higher order.

This theorist Schiller was also a highly practical man. Already through dire need an experienced editor of almanachs, collections and single-handed literary journals, he now wanted to assemble Germany's better-known writers as contributors to a new periodical, *Die Horen* (*Horae*), whose authority would be unquestioned. When, inevitably, its authority was questioned, he became the general in command of a satirical counter-attack which sniped and swiped at nearly every writer and thinker in the land. After that, Schiller settled to producing alongside Goethe the dense succession of his dramas and poems that make Weimar Classicism a shared achievement. The thousand letters they exchanged give a backstage view of this decade of passionate devotion to high aesthetic theory and artistic practice; and they record a friendship which was none the less privately cordial for being centred on a programme of public activity.

'Classicism' implies completed forms, and Goethe's prime imperative after Italy was therefore to finish the works left lying from his first Weimar decade or earlier: the dramas *Egmont, Iphigenie auf Tauris, Torquato Tasso* and *Faust,* and the novel *Wilhelm Meister.* These projects, once completed, virtually are his Classical *œuvre,* which is thus made up not of the artistic conceptions of a ready-made Classicist but of responses to a series of questions left open in his formative years. Meeting this challenge helped to shape his Classical style.

Egmont stays truest to its roots. It is historical drama in the manner of *Götz,* prose—though with subterranean pentameters—in the realistic mode. *Iphigenie* and *Tasso* are in polished verse, confirming along with Schiller's *Don Carlos* that the Shakespearean blank-verse line, if not Shakespeare's grander baroque imagery, was to be the mode of German serious drama.

Iphigenie traces the victory of humane actions over tragic possibilities, and is consequently sometimes dismissed as facile and dated. (We are not supposed to believe in such victories now.) But the dismissal is itself facile, the result of merely juxtaposing Goethe's denouement unimaginatively with routine modern expectations while ignoring the dramatic argument. This is made of fine steel; designed to improve on the ethical crudity of Euripides's version, it can equally well stand up to the clichés of later pessimism.

In Euripides's play, Iphigeneia has been the priestess of Artemis in remote Tauris ever since the goddess rescued her from sacrifice at her father's hands; her brother Orestes has come there to steal the barbarian tribe's image of Artemis as the price set by Apollo for freeing him of the Furies who have pursued him since he murdered his mother. (The sacrifice and the murder are connected phases in the tale of horror which their family has been living through for generations.) Caught in the act of stealing, brother and sister are rescued by Athena from the furious barbarians, who have to put up with the loss of priestess and image for divine purposes.

Goethe takes over this plot as a façade and rebuilds the structure of meaning from within. The ancient black-and-white issue with its wholly unspiritual adventure-story outcome gives way to a subtler alternative which is a spiritual and a practical necessity for Iphigenie. She finally cannot join in robbery. She reveals all to King Thoas, rejecting male stealth and violence and gambling Greek lives on an appeal to a barbarian's humanity. May not people be rendered humane by humane treatment, and does even a barbarian stand outside the circle of humanity and potential nobility? This is very much an eighteenth-century Enlightened idea (cf. Mozart's *Seraglio*), and *Iphigenie* is Goethe's most clearly Enlightenment work. But in Iphigenie herself it is feeling, not philosophy, that directs. She acts from a faith in nobler gods than the other characters are able to conceive, gods who surely cannot want her to do a wrong, and who surely will not allow her and her brother to perish if she does right. When Thoas yields and she has won, it is for her the gods' doing; Orest, too, suddenly sees that the oracle 'really' wanted him to fetch this human sister back from Tauris, not Apollo's sister in effigy (which nicely avoids conflict over who is to have the image). But to the spectator, the outcome seems more the triumph of Iphigenie's human initiative in a dangerously open situation—and thus ultimately of the *dea in anima* that lies behind her actions and replaces Euripides's rescuing *dea ex machina*. The denouement is far from being divinely preordained, but remains touch-and-go till the end.

It is also far from being dated. The arguments of trust and moral initiative are close to those at the heart of the debate over nuclear disarmament. And there is a distinctively feminine, even feminist, logic in Iphigenie's growing unease with her passive role. She reaches the point of ethical breakthrough after repeated subordinations to men: to her father, who would have sacrificed her to get a fair wind for Troy; to King Thoas, who tries to blackmail her into marriage; to her brother and his friend Pylades, who want her to lie as part of their plan. That she will not do this is due not just to the King's past kindnesses, nor (though this is a vital factor reaching out beyond the bounds of the play) because she must keep her hands pure so as to cleanse her family of its age-old curse; it is also because the ills that stretch back through that dark sequence visibly bear the same stamp of largely male impetuosity, of grim action and grim reaction. Her alternative—the logic is unanswerable— is the only hope of breaking out of the sequence.

Yet even as Iphigenie follows her conscience, her doubts and fears make her human in the humbler sense; she is not some kind of moral superwoman, oblivious of the risks she is running. As a serious probing of the ethics of action within a complex web of demands and uncertainties, Goethe's *Iphigenie* leaves most later drama standing. It certainly must not be refused serious attention on the fixed assumption that moral integrity is implausible in literature and ineffectual in life.

In *Iphigenie* individualism (a new ethic) triumphs over the generality (conventional beliefs and tactics) and thereby creates a new generality of principle. The play has common ground, and very nearly a common date, with Kant's categorical imperative, the doctrine that a moral action is one which yields a maxim for all similar situations. *Torquato Tasso* has the same configuration as *Iphigenie*, the individual versus the conventions of a group: a court poet's talent and its associated sensitivities are out of joint with the decorum of social life. That sounds like an echo of Goethe and Weimar, and he did once call the play 'flesh of my flesh and bone of my bone' (E 6 May 1827). If completed when first conceived, it might have been directly autobiographical. But left to time and change, it became a more objective study, first of the (on the whole un-Goethean) historical Tasso; and beyond that of the way any erratic block of 'nature' affects and is affected by the environment which cannot understand it. Instead of being known and taken for what he is and cannot help being, Tasso is nannied, resented, affronted and intrigued over by variously motivated men and women of the Ferrara court. To his patrons he is successively a prized possession, an educable object, an embarrassment and a victim. Only at the very end does one man affirm Tasso's nature for what it is. But by this time he has been cast off by the court; his and our only consolation is his poetic response to fiasco (the present one and its probable successors) which will enrich humanity at his private expense. Yet the social loser in this Chekhovian semi-tragedy has the last word in more than just that poetic sense. The generality has failed to accept the individual for better and worse as a distinctive compound of talents and weaknesses. For all the court's sophistication and Tasso's gaucherie, which the play makes amply clear, it is the generality rather than the individual that stands condemned.

As with *Tasso*, completing the novel *Wilhelm Meister*

involved a shift of attitude to a semi-autobiographical project of the early Weimar years. This time Goethe's changes can be measured, because the original uncompleted text came to light in 1911: *Wilhelm Meister's Theatrical Mission* (*Wilhelm Meisters theatralische Sendung*). Out of this (for its day) remarkably realistic picture of eighteenth-century Germany, Goethe crafted a subtle structure of connections and cross-references and imposed on it the conscious uniformity of a 'pure' style. Out of the serious record of a serious commitment to theatre as a means to social effect (a possibility which the young Goethe's experiences did not rule out) he made a detached, even ironic account of a well-meaning young man who takes a wrong turning in life. Theatre remains the stuff of the story, but the real theme is now character, choice, error, and the chance to learn which error offers.

The hero's ambitions to act and write for the theatre grow from his perception of German society: for him the theatre is the only place where a bourgeois, normally limited to the functions of acquiring and possessing, can move in the freer dimension of simply 'being' and 'appearing' which is the social preserve of the nobility; and for his fragmented country, theatre is to be a means of moral and social cultivation and perhaps even a way towards the community of feeling that might make it a nation. Direct experience of both theatre and nobility leaves the grand notions somewhat battered; a wiser Wilhelm gradually gives up pursuing the total 'harmonious development of my nature' to which he first aspired. Instead he settles for useful self-limitation (he will eventually become a surgeon) within a society which is the only possible form of human totality in modern times.

This may sound a shade moralistic, but the novel is not priggish in tone, or even obtrusively didactic. Direct didacticism has no place in Goethe's Classical programme; and it is the strength of the German *Bildungsroman* or novel of education, of which *Wilhelm Meister* is the true founding text, that the writer need not overtly teach, because he can simply show his central character learning. Wilhelm is shown embracing a great range of experience, social and erotic, in his theatrical adventures. Though he finally turns his back on the theatre, he rejects it not as an object of moral repugnance—even an actress of easy virtue like Philine appears humanly to better advantage than the dutiful bourgeois Werner, who amasses profits by a way of life that is visibly stultifying —but as an illusion he has grown out of.

It may still seem surprising that a Classical artist should describe so extensively a withdrawal from the life of art—especially when his partner Schiller was arguing at exactly this time that art was the one agency independent of social influences which might make divided, specialised man whole again. But Goethe was looking back critically at an actual failure of simplistic ambitions to reshape society directly through the theatre. This was a realistic complement to Schiller's idealistic programme, which in any case had no illusions about the long haul needed ('a task for more than one century') before art could truly restore man. And by concentrating on the making of one socially useful individual, Goethe was addressing the same problem as Schiller. For the central argument of Schiller's *Letters on the Aesthetic Education of Man*, elaborated in response to the Reign of Terror in France, was that there could be no sound political society until beneficent forces had shaped the individuals to compose it. Their 'aesthetic education' did not involve devoting their lives to art; and if Wilhelm Meister is not ideally shaped by his attempt to do that, this again is realistic. It is Goethe's art, in portraying a development in more useful directions, that is calculated to have (true to Schiller's programme) its own long-term effect, not least by its direct appeal to the bourgeois practical ethos. All too much later German— and European—writing was to be art about art and artists, literature about the processes and problems of literature, spinning itself steadily into a cocoon of self-reference from which no substantive butterfly ever emerges. After taking in the artist problem, as far as it has a general point, in *Torquato Tasso*, Goethe sets his face plainly against further artistic introspection in *Wilhelm Meister's Apprenticeship* (*Wilhelm Meisters Lehrjahre*), as it was now called. That is why Novalis, one of the German Romantics who were a major source of the art-about-art tradition, saw Goethe's novel as philistine, a 'Candide against poetry'.

It is on the contrary in total harmony with Goethe's own poetry. For below the theme of turning away from art to practical life, there is the suggestion that Wilhelm's education is a profoundly *natural* process, an unfolding of what is in the character rather than a result of external chance. Much that happens seems fated, even benevolently organised—as often in novels, it turns out to be a small world and a coherent one. Yet these comforting connections are only a quasi-allegorical framework for an inner growth. As ever, the benevolent force of nature is what may aptly be called Goethe's root assumption.

New poetry, inevitably, sprouted vigorously among

the larger works of Goethe's Classicism: hexameters and Classical distich, narratives, elegies, epigrams, didactic poems and ballads. Most ambitiously Classical is the miniature epic *Hermann und Dorothea*, which celebrates the landscape, ethos, occupations and artefacts of the contemporary Rhineland, all illuminated by a brilliant Homeric sun. As is required if idyll is not to be insipid, there is a shadow in the background, cast by the military expansionism of revolutionary France before which Dorothea and her people are fleeing; and there is also much irony, albeit affectionate, in the use of the grand Greek hexametric manner to portray eighteenth-century small-town German bourgeois. Their live counterparts ignored the irony and made this Goethe's most popular work since *Werther*.

The unity of Goethe's Classical *œuvre* lies in the way individuality asserts itself under the even and serene style—not as an arbitrary rebellion against convention, but as the finally unquestionable unfolding of a distinctive personal nature. Even in idyll, with its seemingly bland affirmation of changeless ways, the shy boy Hermann has to find and assert himself before he can marry the refugee girl against his father's sense of bourgeois fitness. Social convention yields to an even stronger and more permanent force; nature is the ever-renewed impulse for change within what seems outwardly changeless.

The Classical Goethe appears as a man at home in a world he has explored and come to understand, in which he can lead a purposeful and immensely productive life—a relative idyll over which immediate shadows fell only in 1805, with Schiller's death, and 1806, with the return of war to North German soil. A decade of persisting and completing in the spirit of a new aesthetic had transformed an inspirational, erratically brilliant poet into a literary master-craftsman. He had met the challenge of his own lines from the 'Prelude on the stage' of *Faust*: 'If you reckon you're a poet,/Order poetry to come' (H 3.15).

But what about *Faust* itself?

4 *Faust*

Northern medieval murk was no place for an avowed Classicist. Committed though Goethe was to the tidying of his pre-Classical desk, it seemed at first more appropriate to abandon this legend of devil-conjuring and soul-selling than to complete it. So in 1790 he published most of what he had written as an avowed fragment (*Faust, ein Fragment*). But the subject was not so easily disposed of. Schiller itched to see the scenes his friend had held back; Goethe himself felt the fascination of the sealed packet. In 1797 he reopened it, added indispensable sections (especially Faust's pact with Mephistopheles), rewrote and restored others, and in 1808 published a relatively rounded text. The Classicist had broken bounds and come to terms with the old Christian cautionary tale.

But this was still only 'The Tragedy, Part One'. Faust had come through the despair, the bargaining, and one shattering episode—his love and destruction of Gretchen; but the consequences of his agreement with Mephisto were far from worked out. Goethe was already thinking of a Second Part, with an arch-Classical motif at its core, the conjuring-up of Helen of Troy; unlike the brief appearance as a court sensation which Marlowe allows her in his *Doctor Faustus*, Goethe's realisation of this episode was to make three massive acts. Yet when he came to execute the plan fully, in the last decade of his life, he was far beyond any single-minded Classicism; the poet who wrote the grand festival of Greek mythological figures that matches the Witches' Sabbath of Part One and introduces Helen was not a doctrinaire Classicist but a virtuoso capable of shaping all cultural materials into equal beauty with equal conviction.

It is an apt irony that the Classicist wrote much of the nordic hocus-pocus, and the post-Classicist that fantastic Greek intermezzo. For *Faust* fits into no neat schema of its author's poetic evolution. It was bigger than any phase, an antidote to all exclusive commitments, a theme round which multifarious materials could accrete, to be treated with a range of techniques that almost empties the poetic cupboard. It was a lifelong challenge to Goethe's imagination. Whatever else is going on at almost any time in his creative life, *Faust* is being planned, gestated, resisted, written, or revised; and when it is finished, the poet dies. It was not so much a composition as a symbiosis.

The result is correspondingly vast. Even English-speaking readers brought up to the wide dramatic freedoms of Shakespeare may find *Faust* hard to grasp—immense in scope (over 12,000 lines), digressive in structure (for long stretches the central dramatic issue seems lost to sight), and often abstruse in detail. All in all, a bizarre monster rather than an obvious masterpiece. It has duly offered scope for endless and sometimes itself bizarre criticism and controversy: for allegorical readings of its characters, its obscurer passages and its overall structure; for minute genetic dissection of the layers of the text; and for fierce debate over whether it finally amounts to a unity. What has never been and cannot be questioned is the unparalleled beauty and power of the poetry. *Faust* is above all a poem rather than a readily practicable stage-drama, increasingly as it proceeds a phantasmagoria for the theatre of the mind—though film might conceivably encompass it. Part One is relatively naturalistic, with its location in 'Gothic'

Germany, a university, a small provincial town. But Part Two is on another plane altogether, a mythic action in the indeterminate space-time of the imagination, Faust himself a mythic embodiment of human impulses who can retrieve Greek Helen from the realm of Persephone and enter into a marriage with her which is also an allegorical union of their cultures. And the brief lifespan of their son commemorates the dead Byron.

This may sound ponderous and 'Germanic', but it is no more ponderous than the myth-play of James Joyce's *Ulysses*, and as much a stylistic *tour de force*. Cultural materials are not plumped down for the reader's dutiful assimilation but displayed and played with for the colour and delight of their shifting facets and cross-connections. 'These very serious jests' was the old Goethe's phrase for his *Faust* (17 March 1832), and 'jests' must be taken as seriously as 'serious'.

But what are the serious themes? What did the legend offer Goethe and what did he make of it? The sixteenth-century German chapbook original, from which Marlowe's *Doctor Faustus* also ultimately derives, was a popular tale of sin and retribution, offering the vicarious thrill of the one and the self-righteous enjoyment of the other. Dr Johann Faust bargains his soul for twenty-four years of Mephisto's service as procurer of pleasure and knowledge. He has his heart's desire and is duly carried off at the end, leaving good Christian readers to shake their heads and be warned as well as satisfied by their glimpse of the illicit. It is a black-and-white story sprung from a black-and-white view of life, for which pleasures of the senses and prying into secret knowledge were in themselves dangerous distractions from man's eternal welfare; to facilitate them by commerce with the devil was perhaps more a difference of degree than of kind.

As once before in *Iphigenie*, where he instilled new meaning into the bargain between Orest and Apollo, Goethe makes a primitive issue complex, this time in an even more complex way. True, Faust appears first as the medieval quester after knowledge, frustrated because academic eminence has brought him no reward but further studious incarceration and because he has exhausted orthodox knowledge without achieving true insight, let alone wisdom. He is desperate to escape from his gloomy Gothic interior, and ripe for the turn to magical means. But before Mephisto is brought on, there is a dazzling prelude which puts him and his conventional devilry permanently in the shade. With the aid of alchemical signs, Faust first attains a vision of the interweaving patterns of the macrocosm and then conjures up the blind amoral force that lies behind them, driving life and death through their tireless cycles: the Earth Spirit. These two conceptions set Goethe's pantheistic imagination alight; what Faust experiences becomes credible in the poetry.

Already the play is rising far above its source-story. The curiosity of a metaphysical peeping Tom has become the burning aspiration of a mind worthy to see into the world's deepest workings. A character whose thirst for and glimpse of that reality can find words such as Goethe gives him cannot be a warning example of evil. The plot has lost its scapegoat and its traditional theme; the pursuit of knowledge has acquired a noble ring, and will surely not be punishable. The superstitions on which the Faust legend was based have failed to survive the Enlightenment—although no Enlightenment writer ever rose to such poetic eloquence to celebrate the spirit of enquiry. Knowledge of the world is validated now not by argument but by beauty.

Goethe

As it happens, a kindly God-the-Father has already told us in a 'Prologue in Heaven' that all will turn out well for Faust in the end, and has licensed Mephisto to do his worst as merely (this is another classic Enlightenment idea) a contributor to the divine plan. Yet this reassuring deity belongs in every sense to another world. He is a conventional figure and the Prologue a pale preliminary which the Classical Goethe later set before those first fiery sequences in his efforts to contain and shape the plot. We 'know' what this scene and figure tell us, but discursively, as information; we know what the Earth Spirit conveys because of the total poetic conviction which the scene and the figure carry.

But the insight into beauty and power is too awesome for Faust, and the Spirit rejects him. With humiliation added to his initial despair, he is a potential client for a lesser figure, the Mephistopheles of the legend. Not surprisingly, Faust is a reluctant buyer, having seen greater things from the Earth-Spirit. Mephisto, all unknowing, still trades in wares that were good enough for a former Faust. From the start the two are at cross purposes. So when Mephisto offers varied pleasures now if Faust will serve him in the afterlife, Faust (who knows and cares nothing about the beyond) can conceive of no pleasure that would ever satisfy his striving mind. He offers a still only half-comprehending Mephisto a wager which entirely reshapes the material of legend. Instead of a man avid for pleasure and ready to squander his soul to secure it, this Faust declares his disbelief that experience could ever be so pleasurable that he would wish to hold on to any fragment of it; and he agrees to let the moment he does so be his last.

Yet with Mephisto's aid he is to plunge with a will into the full range of experiences the world can offer and to expand his being to bursting-point with every kind of human weal and woe. With what aim? Simply that of knowing the typical phenomena of life piecemeal and by accumulation, now that he has been denied the more intimate contact with life's inmost forces glimpsed in the conjuration of the Earth Spirit. It is a vast programme entered into with no illusions, much less any hedonistic appetite. To seize on any one moment as sufficient in its perfection would not merely give Mephisto his triumph in the old dramatic terms (though the word 'soul' has not even been mentioned); more importantly, it would put an end to a pursuit of knowledge which is a theme in its own right—and distinctively Goethean in its stress on the earthly and the individual.

All this is, genetically speaking, late material—the pact scene, like the 'Prologue in Heaven', largely dates from after 1797, and bears the Classical hallmark of the flowing pentameters that have taken over from the deliberately archaic four-beat doggerel of the opening. But in setting the theme of ceaseless movement and activity explicitly to govern the further course of the play, Goethe's version of the pact remains true to those old early scenes in which he had shown the restless Faust reaching out for fullest contact with the world in all its power and complexity. Faust becomes a small human analogue of the Earth Spirit itself, and to that extent in harmony with the underlying reality of things.

The antithesis 'activity–passivity' supplants the legend's antithesis 'good–evil' as the value system behind the action; and its seeming amorality has remained permanently disturbing to readers and critics in a culture with Christian roots. In the pact scene, little sense of evil is left. There are only whiffs of sulphur and hubris, Mephisto demands a signature in Faust's blood (even this is scorned by Faust as pedantry); there is no awareness of sin, in Faust's mind or in anything Mephisto says—his jaunty cynicism belies theological earnestness and masks his grimmer intentions, leaving him a largely comic character.

But Gretchen is different. In her, the tragic victim of Faust's love, sin has all the reality of the legend's own dark period; and in representing her downfall, Goethe does justice as much as Christian dramatist ever did to a suffering which is redoubled by the sufferer's awareness that her soul is separated from God. Having shown with supreme poetic tact the growth of a simple girl's love for a sophisticated stranger, he traces the insidious sequence by which innocent impulses lead to crime and sin: what began as affection ends in accidental murder, infanticide, madness and impending execution. At the end he portrays most movingly a guileless mind, crazed with guilt and fear, yet choosing to embrace earthly punishment and divine judgement rather than flee with the agents of her downfall—the remorseful lover and the eerie companion she has always instinctively shrunk from. In the final prison scene, what is left of Gretchen dwarfs them both, dramatically and morally. As the horses for her escape wait vainly, shivering in the first light, the impatient Mephisto cries out 'She is doomed!' But he is answered by a voice from above, and Gretchen's conviction of sin by an equally orthodox divine mercy, with the words 'Is saved!'

Such orthodoxy only matches and serves Goethe's own Classical inclination. He added the rescuing words in the late 1790s because he clearly found their absence intolerable, just as he reshaped the whole scene in verse because he found the stark naturalistic prose of the original version intolerable. So he was being a little disingenuous when in later years he replied to criticisms from the orthodox: 'Me heathen? I had Gretchen executed and I let Ottilie starve away [we shall meet her later], isn't that Christian enough for people? What do they want more Christian than that?' (H 6.623). For he was no Christian artist and even Gretchen is not a figure of Christian art; she is a Christian figure created by the highest secular art, embraced by the compassion of an art to which nothing human is foreign.

Thematically she remains nevertheless in some measure a foreign element in Goethe's secularised treatment of the legend, a deeply moving dissonance. Structurally too her tragedy as a dramatic episode fits imperfectly into the overall scheme the pact lays down. It is of course possible to see her as one of the pleasures with which Mephisto tries to satisfy Faust; and Faust's first reaction to her—'Listen, you must get me the girl!'—suggests this. (It suggests, indeed, that he is much more the traditional pursuer of pleasure than Goethe's pact scene allows—and perhaps, when this much earlier scene was written, he still was.) But his lust quickly becomes love, carrying him far beyond Mephisto's range; devilish tactics with an eye to the pact are forgotten, and the episode turns into a complete mini-ature bourgeois love-tragedy—'miniature' only in its relative brevity. Perhaps only Faust's abandoning of Gretchen, heartless and never expressly motivated in the text, can be read as an act of obedience on both his and Goethe's part to the imperative of the pact: that Faust shall move on to new experiences. But even this is to reinterpret from the standpoint of the finished text something which is as it is for originally quite different reasons. The story of an abandoned girl was an early and chance accretion to a *Faust* project already in progress, an immediate response to the horror of just such an infanticide and ritual public beheading which occurred in Frankfurt in the mid-1770s when Goethe was a young lawyer there. Certainly the pressure of such an experience would help to explain the extreme intensity of feeling at the painful high-points of the action—Gretchen's terror in the cathedral when she is caught between a tormenting evil spirit and the savagery of the 'Dies irae'; Faust's reviling of Mephisto for his part in corrupting her; and the final harrowing scene in Gretchen's cell. Even more, it would explain why Goethe suddenly concentrated so totally, to the point of completing it, on this one episode out of a much larger and only very patchily executed conception. It looks as if this larger work and its male lead (ill suited though Faust was to play the romantic hero before his professorial persona had been cast off in a rejuvenation scene) were commandeered to meet a pressing emotional and dramatic need. In both respects, emotional intensity and prompt completion, the Gretchen tragedy stands out in the total geology of *Faust*: it is volcanic, not sedimentary.

The impartial art that embraces Gretchen with its compassion does not rush to damn Faust, extreme though his guilt is in simple human terms. Or perhaps rather, the structure of the whole work grows beyond the immediate relevance of such condemnation. Simply from the closing lines of Part One in Gretchen's cell, it would be just possible to think that Mephisto is carrying Faust off. But by the terms of the pact Goethe has subsequently devised, it can only be to further adventures. And if the episodic plan is indeed to be followed as the basis for Part Two, then in some respects the slate has to be wiped clean. Guilt from an earlier episode will not connect with the issues of the next one. The epic structure needs a Faust character that will focus the issues of the pact (which do persist) in successive contexts, but not show a coherent moral consciousness. Faust duly begins Part Two with the gift of magical oblivion—a secular absolution; he is a mythic character, with the enlarged scope but also the limitations that entails.

With the central figure larger yet humanly paler, the experiences in store for him can take on an almost self-sufficient interest; and with the play's whole status similarly raised from a human drama containing some magic elements to an action licensed in its entirety by magic to range over myth and history, Goethe can give imaginative realisation to whatever fascinates him as an object of human striving. So if the Faust who was lukewarm about Mephisto's proffered pleasures now becomes eager, to the point of obsession, in the pursuit of Helen, it is because he is re-enacting his author's enthusiasms. A drama which has already become epic by its structure thus becomes virtually lyrical in its function, and thereby—on the grandest scale—continues a process begun long before when the young Goethe's impatience for ultimate knowledge, and his intuition of where it might be found, spoke lyrically through the mask of Faust.

This does not make the work a mere versified résumé of Goethe's spiritual involvements. Faust's impulse is always more important than its object, the movement more than the goal. But this itself creates a problem, or rather it brings out a problem which was always inherent in Goethe's conception of the pact. As Faust moves on, from the aesthetic–sexual idyll of his marriage to Helen (where he comes near to declaring the satisfaction he is pledged never to feel, though not in the set wording of the pact—and Mephisto is apparently a literal-minded devil) to imperial politics, land-reclamation, colonising and trade, the question becomes pressing: how can such *endless* striving be represented in a necessarily finite work? Which is only the artistic side of a more basic difficulty: how can the wager (supposing Mephisto is not to be the winner) ever be conclusively won?/ How can Faust ever achieve the positive purpose which is the other aspect of his never being satisfied, namely the accumulation of knowledge through successive experiences?/There will always be more world than he can know. Mephisto meanwhile has presumably all the time in eternity; Faust might lose if he were to weaken, but he can never *finally* win by remaining firm. Has Goethe from the first backed a poetic loser?

On the contrary. When Faust is saved, it is quite specifically a poetic victory, flowing as a general wisdom from Goethe's practice as a poet. Faust does finally speak the fateful words that bid one beautiful moment stay, but to a moment of vision, not of sensuous pleasure. Blinded, guilt-laden more than ever, aged and—having abjured magic—near to natural death, he foresees the never-ending labours that will be needed to hold the ground he has reclaimed. He savours not the 'paradisal' land for itself (idyll is not enough) nor any noble communal effort (he is not a social idealist), but simply the balance of challenge and response between the threatening sea and human effort, the maintaining of which must stretch endlessly into the future. His vision concentrates that sequence and its value in a single moment, a symbolic moment therefore in the way poetry, and Goethe's poetry especially, uses symbol: →setting the concrete for the abstract, the moth round the candle-flame for man's aspiration beyond mortal limits (H 2.18), or a single day's precisely observed course and serene sunset for his own fulfilled life (H 1.391)—seeing, in Blake's phrase, eternity in a grain of sand. That is true symbolism, where the particular represents the more general, not as dream or shadow but as the living and instant revelation of what lies beyond investigation (H 12.471). Like the dot that marks the recurring decimal, Faust's visionary speech is a sufficient notation for the endless activity he remains committed to but which the play could never have exhaustively presented.

Having spoken the formula, Faust duly dies. Mephisto, hearing only the stipulated words—'Verweile doch, du bist so schön!'—and not their subtler sense, does not understand why this seemingly empty moment has provoked them, nor why he himself seems to have lost the wager—for Faust's 'immortal part' (only the traditionalist Mephisto calls it his 'soul') is borne up to heaven. Thus the cross-purposes between a legend-true Mephisto and a transformed Faust persist to the very end. Heaven too is transformed. It is no longer the static place the Lord inhabited in the Prologue, but a place of sublime heights and depths where the movement and progression of earth remain possible. It is presided over by the Virgin-in-Glory (the Lord has vanished altogether, and Christ never was in evidence); while to intercede with her on Faust's behalf and draw him on to further heights, closing Part Two in serenity as she closed Part One in tragedy, there is a penitent once known as Gretchen.

Despite the iconography, this is no orthodox salvation, and Goethe has undergone no belated conversion. He manipulates Christian motifs, so he told Eckermann, in order to express concretely what would otherwise have risked being vague and intangible (E 6 June 1831). The ending in heaven and the familiar devotional figure are an allegorical affirmation of Faust. The discrepancy between the two heavens which frame the action shows how little Goethe was concerned with doctrine and belief and how little he cared—even to the point of artistic negligence—about unifying the mythical materials which at different stages served his various purposes.

So what is the meaning of Faust's 'salvation'? The dicta of the scenes in heaven at opposite ends of the work compose a message: that all human striving entails error, but that (more importantly) the natural impulse underlying it springs from an obscure intuition of the right path; that Faust's course is in some sense guided; and that to persist in honest striving, however much error (and consequently tragedy) is entailed, may be enough to satisfy the ultimate authorities. All in all, it is a justification of natural man and of a progress through life which, however unregenerate, can still be affirmed. It reminds us that Goethe had dismissed Kant's late theory of the 'radical evil' in man as an unworthy relapse into the kind of superstition the great philosopher and the Enlightenment as a whole had laboured to remove (7 June 1793). But Goethe's conception goes beyond the Enlightenment idea of a potential in man that is somehow 'meant' to be worked out in the world; and it drops the moral connotations of that idea in favour of a sheer vigour of entelechy that carries beyond death, seeming not so much to be transformed for the transcendent world as to invade transcendence with earthly energies. It appropriates the Christian's deepest faith that life is in beneficent hands, but the beneficiary is an undeserving character in Christian terms, as indeed in the terms of any rigorous morality. It is all as far from the spirit of the original Faust story as it is possible to get.

So is it wisdom in Goethe to suggest that to a divinely broad mind all human guilt would appear as error? Or is it presumption? Is it sufficient to offer activity as the defining characteristic of humankind and a higher ideal than moral guiltlessness? Is it a philosophically mature resignation to accept the tragic consequences of human action because they are necessarily entwined with that vital principle? Or is it a dangerous laxity, parallel in individual ethics to Hegel's apologia of this same decade for ruthlessness on the larger stage of history? However these questions are answered which have always disturbed readers of *Faust*, the idea that activity is man's defining characteristic, and that its tireless continuation has an intrinsic value even before we consider its particular goals, is a challenging newcomer among the great themes of literature. It may have been present as a strand in other, traditional, themes; that man should restlessly pursue truth, or the fulfilment of his potential, rather than complacently possess it, is an idea found in more than one Enlightenment thinker. But to have made it explicit and given it centre-stage in a great poem is part of Goethe's originality. It is the logical conclusion of the explorations and intuitions which began in the poems of a 'very earthly' young man.

Goethe's monumental treatment of the theme stands challengingly at a pivotal point in history. It questions the assumptions of virtually all the philosophies and theologies of the past, according to which human nature was 'being', a changeless essence whose residence on earth only temporarily and regrettably involved it in transient 'doing' and other forms of change. These things were allegedly a mere husk from which the essence would in due course be liberated into a higher realm—a static, once-and-for-all heaven; nirvana; oneness with some fixed ideal. Against this Goethe sets the idea of man's nature as inherently 'doing'; this and its associated forms of change—movement, development, growth —are not mere preliminaries or obstacles to the attaining of his true nature, they *are* that nature. Man is a creature of time and the world, not a refugee from them. In this dynamic and anti-transcendent conception, the long haul of humanist individualism which began again in the Renaissance after centuries-long interruption achieves the full confidence of its convictions.

Less obviously, but with equal historical aptness, Goethe's definition of man's nature and needs as lying in activity rather than enjoyment comments on new assumptions that arose in his time and have largely governed Western society since. Acquisitiveness no doubt always was a prominent feature of man; but the new forces of industrial expansion were beginning to concentrate the mind and energies of Europe more and more exclusively on the production and consumption of material goods. The processes involved might seem dynamic enough—the harnessing of the required mechanical power, the multiplying of manufactured objects; and certainly they reached out with their effects far beyond the European continent. But the idea they implied that human fulfilment need only consist in accumulation or repetitive consumption was static and stultifying, an equivalent of the satiety which was all the Faust of legend could achieve, with the Industrial Revolution now playing the role of Mephisto and a seemingly inexhaustible world of natural resources at its command. It would have been an inadequate idea of fulfilment even if the material means to it had been more widely and justly distributed.

Against it Goethe sets his image of man as impatiently transcending gratification, pursuing instead goals which recede and change as he moves and which, if they were ever to afford satisfaction, would somehow have to preserve—as Faust's last vision does—the feel of the pursuit itself. For the pursuit *is* the goal, man is defined by movement. This goes further than the old Aristotelean definition of happiness as lying in the pursuit of worthwhile goals, and singles out the element of continual striving as the source of value in that process. It provides the ultimate term of comparison for Hegel's and Marx's concepts of alienation; and it remains relevant and thought-provoking now that industrial processes need less and less of the human energies they once monopolised, so that people may yet be free, in a rethought society, to follow activities that will be ends in themselves and to achieve growth of more than just the economic kind.

5 Variations

If it was a mark of Goethe's creative power to have achieved his own Classicism, it is a mark of his range and resilience that he then grew beyond it, at least in externals. He had more to say, and he was attracted to more diverse themes and materials, than would fit into strictly Classical forms. *Faust* showed that. And true to the Faustian principle, Classicism proved to have been one moment of balance in a continuing movement.

External forces played a part, demanding change. Goethe's Classicism had been a normative statement of order in an age of revolution and war which for a time, and from a distance, it was possible to view as an episode. In a group of largely satirical plays and fragments of the 1790s Goethe had treated revolution as a curable or, outside France, preventable phenomenon. These works fall short of the realities of the time by trivialising the causes of unrest and caricaturing the motives of revolutionaries. The trouble was that for Goethe violent events could not appear in any sense historically legitimate because he believed that all 'real' processes must be rhythmic natural developments. Even in geology he was a Neptunist, believing that the earth's crust was shaped by the gradual action of water, against the Vulcanists who believed in the sudden action of fire. True, his sober eye saw some of what was going on in France more clearly than his easily enthused contemporaries; he wrote caustic epigrams on the power-hungry ideologues and the new tyranny which the people were getting in exchange for the old, as well as on the deserved discomfiture of the *ancien régime*. But his jaundiced attitude of 'plus ça change, plus c'est la même chose' missed seeing the fundamental change beneath the surface turbulence and politicking.

'Change' meant more than just war, which came unpleasantly close in 1806, or new political forms. Since the Revolution everything in Europe had seemed open to question, the overthrow of an old order and the new start in politics were merely the surface signs of deeper stirrings. As war engulfed the Continent, younger German poets and thinkers sniffed the air hopefully, sensing some barely definable millennium that would surely follow the necessary destruction. Morality, community, religion would be fundamentally renewed. A new art and a new literature, even a new mythology, would arise from these profound changes or actually contribute to them. What had begun in France was irreversible and it had opened up limitless expectations.

But an older poet—Goethe was forty when the Revolution happened—could not trust vague expectations and did not want limitless instability. He had forged his order from nature, art and cultural history; it had yielded rich poetic results and could be expected to go on doing so. When Schiller's death deprived him of his Classical partner, he felt unable to make a new start. He might well have persisted in a Classicism more and more deliberate and against the grain of the times, turning in on himself and increasingly formalising his aesthetic credo. There had already been signs of a Classicistic pedantry in the subjects and treatment he chose for himself (especially *Achilleis*, a fragmentary attempt to create pastiche Homer in German) or recommended to others. Yet remaining true to his established Classical self would have meant falling behind the young writers who were ready to embrace chaos and to experiment with new forms and ideas. It would also have meant being untrue to his deepest principle—growth—which was what made his Classicism a live force in the first place. It had been evolved in response to the world as he found it, not arbitrarily imposed; a changing world was not to be shut out in its name.

So 1805 was a turning-point, though doubtless Goethe never thought through the issues in this form, any more than he could be aware how varied a creativity—twenty-seven years of it—was to be made possible by returning to an open-ended dialectic with the world. At all events, within four years he had produced a novel which goes so far towards meeting turmoil on its own shifting ground that the Goethe of a few years before would not have countenanced it, let alone written it. On the surface, *Elective Affinities* (*Die Wahlverwandtschaften*) is calm enough. Society is not seen in travail, indeed society at large is not seen at all: everything takes place on one secluded country estate between four main characters, a married couple, a male friend, a young girl. Pairs part and recombine in the way some natural elements do ('elective affinities' is the name chemists of the day gave this process). Are human beings merely natural elements too, helpless automata through whom nature works? That the new couples are 'made for each other' is plain from repeated bizarre manifestations, not least when a chance intercourse between the married pair produces a child resembling both absent lovers. In a circle that has plainly given up ethical absolutes, pursuing natural inclination must seem the best, even the only, remaining course. But things are not left to work out with permissive symmetry. Just when the last obstacle to divorce and remarriages is removed by the accidental death of the child, the youngest partner, Ottilie, refuses to proceed: the death she was involved in has stirred her sense of guilt. This is not a hearking back to the old morality—she has all along been a strangely unconventional and unworldly figure; it is an instinct. She has strayed from 'her' path, transgressed 'her' law. She denies herself the man she loves, denies all their fulfilments, turns to saintly asceticism and virtually starves herself to death. She becomes an 'earthly saint' (5 May 1810).

This may seem a strange outcome from the poet of sensuous well-being who had been living harmoniously in a benevolent natural world. But what he is facing is the darker realm of mysterious forces which the speculations of his younger Romantic contemporaries had opened up; they were fascinated precisely by its darkness after so much Enlightenment and more concerned to revel in it than to map it. Goethe does not revel in it, he explores it to the point where an individual under the strongest of compulsions suddenly reacts, asserts herself in an unexpected direction and draws a moral answer from her own inner resources. The younger generation had spoken airily of a new morality; Goethe shows one actually being created. Of course, it is not entirely new. It has recognisable roots in the individualism which he had always held to; Iphigenie is Ottilie's ancestor, and Goethe has once more, in the paradoxical phrase George Eliot used of his *Wilhem Meister*, 'waited patiently for the moral processes of nature' to operate. But he has ventured well outside his old secure terrain to do so, and has managed to find balance and reconciliation again, though of a tragic kind.

He has also been speaking, through issues that seem intimately private, about society and its disarray as it

finds that the old moral maps lack authority and that
there is no putting the clock back to the time when they
were an adequate guide. His analysis is the more
effectively disquieting for being indirect. The early
chapters, with a couple shaping and reshaping the
landscape of their estate but never quite agreeing how,
already subtly suggest a disturbance of society that
reaches down to its natural roots, and a loss of confident
direction. The actors' responses to the chemistry of their
passions, ranging from eager acceptance of nature's
dictates via hollow rule-conformity to the extreme of
Ottilie's obstinate self-abnegation, show a fibre of
character that by implication other, larger dilemmas
would similarly reveal. The narrative only ceases to be
representative of the way contemporary men and women
would behave when it reaches Ottilie, who is a model
rather than a reflection. Not for the last time in
European literature, the disharmonies of marriage and
sexual attraction have been made to convey essentials
about society which might have eluded explicit discussion.

Goethe uses them again a year later in what seems at
first sight a frivolous vein. The narrator in the comic
verse-tale 'Das Tagebuch' (The Diary), staying far from
home and true love, invites a servant-girl to his inn
room. There is no obstacle to his pleasure—except that
he finds himself unable. Never before has he been
incapacitated by tiredness or inhibition, the organ he
calls by the quaint neologism 'Master Iste' has never yet
let him down. Now he is left silently cursing, with the
girl innocent and intact asleep beside him. As she sleeps,
his normal powers return, but only through thoughts of
the woman he has loved since his young days and to
whom he is (now in the fullest sense) returning. Love

rather than duty has kept him faithful, the organism has itself controlled his behaviour. Such is the potency of a natural morality—or the morality of a natural impotence. The poem could superficially be taken for salacious rococo, and no doubt would have been if Goethe had published it in his lifetime. But beneath the rueful man-of-the-world humour, there is another serious exploration of his characteristic alternative to all dualistic (e.g. Kantian) struggles of moral reason against natural impulse.

Something like the delicate symbolic tactics of *Elective Affinities* recurs in the brief late tale simply called *Novelle* (*Novella*). It is a fable about rule and self-rule, which links the violent forces in nature (fire) with those in man (passion, impetuous destructiveness) and sets against them counter-motifs of restraint: natural piety and the Daniel-like gentleness with which the child and his song recapture an escaped lion, so that the alternative of killing it appears in all its contrasting crudity.

As against such allusive indirectness, the resumed story of Wilhelm Meister, the *Years of Travel* (*Wilhelm Meisters Wanderjahre*) treats social themes head on: feudalism, old crafts undermined by mechanisation; emigration to America as a possible new start; and education, for which an ideal system is sketched in a utopian 'pedagogical province'. There are also substantial sections of weighty aphorisms. The framework narrative of Wilhelm's progress and the sometimes brilliant short stories inset in it cannot remove the impression that this is a book of wisdom rather than a work of fiction. It is not easy to read *Wilhelm Meister's Years of Travel* as a novel, even allowing for the reflectiveness of the German *Bildungsroman* tradition. So that in this work we really do reach 'Goethe the Sage'—though not till 1829, only three years before his death. And if there is a temptation to say that here at last, in his prose, he has grown old and somewhat ponderous, his poetry is as dynamic as ever.

At sixty-five a new and sustained inspiration had set him off writing poems in emulation of the fourteenth-century Persian lyricist Hafiz. They range over almost every subject and mood—erotic (he is in love again), bibulous, polemical, historical, reflective. Reflection and evocation sometimes have an almost mystical intensity, as past insight and experience are concentrated in fresh perceptions of beauty. The poet can see the woman he loves in every shape and stimulus of the sensible world, much as the Muslim believer names Allah in a hundred forms. In loving her, he loves the world and whatever god is immanent in it; none of these loves is merely a derivate of any other, they compose a single embracing reverence. The Goethe of the *West-eastern Divan* (*West-östlicher Divan*) has been well called a 'mystic without a religion'.

He also discovers a sense of unity across historical time. When Goethe began writing his Persian poems, it was partly as an escape from the surrounding chaos of Napoleon's last phase. But the depths of the Eastern past showed him similar phenomena: the same wars, the same great conquerors (Napoleon 'recurs' as Tamburlaine), the same threats to life and happiness, the same causes of anger and distress. Yet also, in Hafiz and his songs, the same necessity—and possibility—for love and poetry to thrive in adverse circumstances. Even more strongly than in the *Roman Elegies*, where he claimed kinship with his Latin predecessors, life resolves itself into archetypes. Even so, the freshness and value of each new occasion stays intact. Archetype, recurrence, myth—the perspective they offer never blurs or attenuates the single instance. Great poetry can combine repetition and uniqueness, the pattern and the piece, so that they enrich each other.

Goethe's Persian poems are not just pastiche and ironic play. He adapts the exotic mode to his deepest purposes, as he does again in the late cycle *Chinese-German Days and Seasons (Chinesisch-deutsche Jahres- und Tageszeiten)*, or yet again in *Faust II* when he returns to the materials of Greek and Christian culture —but now as a traveller from more distant places, for whom these have become merely two among the many components of world literature. (The term 'world literature', incidentally, was Goethe's coining—H 12.352 f., 361 f.)

So his is something rather different from the ironic modern consciousness which Hegel diagnosed in his *Aesthetics* as no longer able to create convincing form because it was no longer absorbed by belief in the figures and myths it had to work with. That account fitted some of his Romantic contemporaries, and incidentally helped to explain why they drifted back to the old Church when the all-transforming 'new religion' failed to materialise. But it does not fit Goethe and his remarkable power of assimilation, in the sense both of integrating new materials into his vision and of shaping his entire range of thought and feeling to new modes. If his choice of materials and medium was 'free', it led on to total—artistic—absorption. In a phrase of Novalis's, he 'works in religion' (and by the same token in other, less highly charged materials) 'as a sculptor works in bronze'. In substance and in form, Goethe's late work is catholic, versatile, virtuoso.

Ageing brought further perspectives. Writing his auto-biographical works—*Poetry and Truth*, which covered the years up to 1775, *Italian Journey* (*Italienische Reise*), and *Campaign in France* (*Campagne in Frank-reich*)—brought the phases of his own life into historical relief; seeing his past against a broad background of time and events, he 'became historical' to himself. He even attributes a similar sense of perspective to his past self, claiming to have seen a historical turning-point in the cannonade with which the French revolutionary citizens' army drove back the German princes at Valmy in 1792, and to have told other onlookers: 'From this day and place a new epoch of world history is beginning, and you can say that you were there' (H 10.235). But besides all this his poetic works now constitute a history, a rich past of their own. So when love and loss afflict him again at seventy-four, the crises of his earlier figures structure his response; he can invoke Werther's shade and fatal despair as he broods over his new misery, but then be led on to Tasso's consolation, seeking relief of pain by forcing himself to remember and recount every detail of what he suffered. Multiple emotion recollected is a means to tranquillity. Once more Goethe has done something the Romantics dreamed about: created a new mythology. But where they proposed bizarre mixtures of science, philosophy, European literature and legend and oriental myth, he has built one from motifs of his own making. In the gloomy *Trilogy of Passion* (*Trilogie der Leidenschaft*), it shapes and mitigates the unprece-dented outburst of feeling, it bears the poetic weight put on it, it works.

The *Trilogy* marks a relapse into particular desire at a time when Goethe had long assigned love its place in a considered scheme along with the other moving forces of life—the individual daimon, chance, compulsion, hope, all scrutinised in the grandiose terse stanzas of the poem 'Primal Words. Orphic' ('Urworte. Orphisch') —and at an age when fulfilment was scarcely a part of the permanent pattern of existence that he could hope to relive. The whole incident seems an anachronism, an embarrassment; yet it is also, through the havoc it wreaks in his life, a sublime reminder that the wisdom of patterns and archetypes is not proof against the attack of raw experience.

Still, the attack of the single instance cannot be sustained long against the structure Goethe had built up; disappointment, however bitter, could not undo a lifetime's satisfactions. The *Trilogy* is one of the rare moments in Goethe's work when darkness for a time overcomes light, but it is brief.

As Goethe grows very old, the light seems—strangely— to get brighter. The conviction of a coherent, benevolent world persists, not to be overshadowed by thoughts of destruction and decay. In 1829 the clearing of a Weimar churchyard brought Schiller's skull back into the light after it had lain in the earth for the same span as Yorick's. But Goethe's musings as he holds it in his hands and remembers the man are quite unlike Hamlet's: not abhorrence at the thought of past familiarity with what is now decomposed, but exhilaration at having known the power of mind and eloquence that flowed through this bone receptacle, which is only one from an ocean of created and creative forms. The grand terza rimas commemorate Schiller as an example of the 'God-Nature' which it is life's greatest gain to know; in the cold narrow charnel-house, the poet feels:

Free and refreshed, suffused with glowing warmth,
As if a source of life from death came springing.

(Daß in des Raumes Moderkält' und Enge
Ich frei und wärmefühlend mich erquickte,
Als ob ein Lebensquell dem Tod entspränge.)

(H 1.366)

So near to his own death, Goethe can still turn the classic 'memento mori' of reflections on a death's head into a 'memento vivere'.

Here and in all his late poetry, the language is unadorned, things and processes are named in plain, often abstract words; yet the abstraction is belied by a strong sense of concreteness, of visualised essence. Like the syntax, which without being intricate achieves great concentration by stating only essentials, the subjects are themselves essentials, the basic processes of the world and the universe—making and unmaking, individuation and transformation, the constant change and movement that compose eternal calm. For the old poet, as a lifelong observer of nature and explorer of new ways to shape words to things, what is left is to state the essence of all he has seen, as concisely and compellingly as he can, and then fall silent in wonder (H 1.358).

It makes sense that Goethe published this final poetic summa in his scientific journals. Not that scientists now would be likely to recognise his visionary mode as science. But the vision derives from his years of scientific study and has its roots in the principles of metamorphosis, wholeness and continuity that informed all his scientific theorising and model-building. It is true that there was a good deal wrong (as we saw) with the way the principles were applied in some areas, and with the detail even of those theories which pioneered in the right general direction. Yet the principles and the vision, and with them these late poems, still have a persuasiveness—an essence of their own—which is not easily undermined. Freud once wrote that a paranoiac is right about many things but wrong about everything. Of Goethe and his picture of the world it is possible to feel that the reverse is true.

6 'A happy constellation'

In *Poetry and Truth* Goethe records that the heavenly bodies at his birth stood 'in a happy constellation', and this was perhaps why he survived at all: 'For through the midwife's clumsiness I came into the world as if dead, and only repeated efforts brought it about that I saw the light.'

The picture of life triumphing—just—over death is an apt beginning to an existence which strikes us as supremely happy and harmonious, yet without being vapidly unproblematic. The forces from which Goethe had to shape his personal order and his works were no less great than other men have to face and were perhaps greater, starting with the almost pathological excitability and volatility of his early youth. There were tragic possibilities in him, sometimes realised in his works. Age and wisdom never made him blandly serene, and throughout his life dark moods are recorded by those who observed him. He told the friend of his later years, the musician Zelter, that he felt quite capable of writing a second *Werther* which would make people's hair stand on end (3 Dec. 1812). Even where his poetry is at its most exuberant and exhilarating, it has the grain of a worked reality, not the smoothness of facile optimism.

'Optimism' nevertheless, in some richer and more complex sense, remains an unavoidable term. Why should we feel awkward about using it? Only because since Goethe's day pessimism and nihilism have become the dominant cultural mode and virtually a qualification for being taken seriously. Few of the writers who

compose the modern canon have given a positive overall
view of the human condition and the world man lives in.
Yet Goethe too belongs to the modern period in the
broadest cultural sense—the period in which the decline
of accepted beliefs sent every authentic self out to
explore the world as it appeared to fresh eyes. Goethe's
explorations were among the first and greatest examples
of this process; but he pushes on beyond the general
instability and reaches firm ground again. He finds that
the world is good (at its natural base, that is—society is
too variable a factor to be relied on) and his sense of
nature's goodness is more than just the private gratitude
of a favoured being.. His perceptions claim general
validity: they are at once richer and more coherent (he is
a great poet), more precise and informed (he is a
scientist), more extensive and repeated (he is eventually
an old man) than most people's. They demand to be
taken seriously even if they differ from a later cultural
consensus.

That they do so differ, and compose an unfashionably
positive image of life, has one main reason: not the
exclusion of unpleasant elements, but a balancing
inclusion of the positive elements which the pessimistic
consensus has increasingly ignored. This is a conscious
position from quite early on. In 1782 Goethe received a
letter of unhappy self-analysis from his Christian friend
Lavater. He replied that any such account must tend
towards imbalance, which the reader has to allow for by
a 'special psychological calculation' in order to get a true
picture. The mechanics of the imbalance are explained
thus:

> What a man notices and feels about himself seems to
> me the least part of his existence. He is struck more

by what he lacks than by what he possesses, he notices more what causes him anxiety than what delights him or expands his mind; for in all good and pleasant states, the mind loses awareness of itself, as the body does too, and is only reminded of itself again by unpleasant sensations; and so for the most part someone writing about himself and his past condition will note down whatever is painful and constricting; by which process, if I can put it like this, a person is bound to shrink. (4 Oct. 1782)

This points up Goethe's own achievement in keeping present to his and our minds the 'pleasant states' of existence—in the broadest possible sense—which a preoccupation with its pains may edge out. It also diagnoses prophetically the modern literature of 'Angst' (the concept is already contained in Goethe's reference to 'anxiety' and 'constriction') and, by implication, the way such writing may come to dominate: not because suffering is necessarily in itself more important, or more profound; nor because modern experience is more tragic than that of past ages (how could one begin to quantify that?) but at least in part because of the technical difficulty of achieving balanced perception and representation. Pain is more obtrusive and presses for utterance more urgently than those pleasant states; in a sense, it is easier to write about than they are. Any interspersed happiness then goes by default, and the false conclusion is gradually drawn (supported by those trivial works of vacuous idyll or kitsch which do treat it) that happiness is too banal a theme, too featureless an experience to be worth attending to at all. The view is shared by the recent (1983) Nobel prizewinner for literature, and apparently also, as a principle of choice, by the Nobel selection committee.

Such a belief is epitomised by the opening of Tolstoy's *Anna Karenina*: 'All happy families are like one another; every unhappy family is unhappy in its own way.' But is it true that happy families are any more uniform than unhappy ones? Or is it simply that the nuances of happiness are harder to render (though the Tolstoy of *War and Peace* rendered a fine variety), just as the unobtrusive phenomenon of happiness generally is harder to render than the dramatic phenomenon of suffering? That would be no index of their relative importance, much less desirability, as literary themes. And if happiness and its nuances are not rendered adequately, they will fade from sight altogether beside the sharper profile of misery. It is too much to expect that the reading public will apply to the works which build up our collective consciousness the kind of special calculation that Goethe said was needed in order to offset the emphasis of Lavater's gloomy letter. As a consequence, the 'shrunken' image of human experience insidiously becomes the norm—for new writers, for the judgement of literature, for the perception of life itself; and the norm becomes increasingly difficult to be critically aware of and to escape from.

All this is not to question the authenticity of much modern (and ancient) writing which has pessimistic implications, nor is it to dismiss the unhappy families of literature, from the Tantalids to the Alvings and Samsas. But it is to question the *necessity* of pessimism, whose exclusive claims may be a literary fashion rather than a permanent truth. It would of course make no sense to tell the authentic pessimist, the writer genuinely oppressed with his or others' suffering, to look on the bright side—literary expression is inherently subjective. Yet even here it is relevant that the direction of Goethe's whole development, and eventually his conscious aim, was precisely to limit subjectivity and open the mind to experience, extending to every sphere the principle Francis Bacon stated in respect of human learning, namely that

> the wit and mind of man, if it work upon matter, which is the contemplation of the creatures of God, worketh according to the stuff and is limited thereby; but if it work upon itself, as the spider worketh his web, then it is endless, and brings forth cobwebs . . . admirable for the fineness of thread and work, but of no substance or profit.

Goethe's answer to Lavater already implies a notion of objectivity, though not as a simple contrary term to subjectivity. Rather, it is something wider which embraces subjective awareness: there is a larger self which is narrowed and misrepresented by selective absorption in its ills. Such self-absorption is the way to *Weltschmerz* and Werther, and beyond that to the sometimes self-indulgent introspection of the high Romantic era (the stress on misery and suffering here at issue is quite distinct from the awareness of social misery that produces critical and committed writing). The opposite path leads—and led Goethe—to a grasp of the whole self as a part of the real world. Objectivity as he achieved it in and after Italy does not mean merely 'accurate seeing'; it means maximum absorption in external things, so that reality can determine and balance the observer's mental processes. Looking at Roman buildings he felt himself, in that strangely literal phrase for what the world could do to the mind, 'become solid'.

Whether Goethe ignored Kant's argument that ultimate reality is inaccessible and all experience a mental construct, or whether he took it for granted and began undaunted from that universal human starting-point, his mature outlook rests on just that: looking outward. He expressly rejects the Delphic injunction 'Know thyself!' as 'a ruse of conspiring priests to confuse men by unattainable demands and to tempt them away from acting on the external world to a false inner contemplation. Man only knows himself in so far as he knows the world, which he only perceives in himself and himself in it' (H 13.38). If he seeks knowledge of and through the world, then 'every new object, properly considered, opens up a new organ in us'—a far cry from plunging into the abyss of an insubstantial ego. It is this, rather than the use of ancient myth and metre, that makes Goethe a Classicist in a Romantic age. He is one of the 'few people who possess an imagination for the truth of the real' (E 25 Dec. 1825). The works that result offer a solid counter-image to the Romantic imagination of his day and to the darker imaginings that have followed since.

But is Goethe's optimism not itself in some measure self-indulgent, the nonchalance of a successful and happy man in a partly unhappy world? And is reading him not a self-indulgence in its turn? Is the invitation to affirm existence perhaps simply another kind of 'ruse to tempt men away from acting on the external world', and Goethe's whole work part of the affirmative culture which goes with social quietism?

Certainly Goethe is part of 'official' culture, and has been so ever since nineteenth-century Germans misread his deep sense of order as a model for social conformity. More recently, Germans with a developed political consciousness and conscience have rejected him as an establishment figure, in his own time and in his subsequent effects. But the question is more complex than they have allowed. Affirmation of life is not necessarily conformist, any more than anxiety-ridden negations are necessarily ideal sources of healthy social influence. To say it again, Goethe's affirmation was only ever of the natural world, not the social world; and nature, at least since Rousseau, has been the great counter-image and challenge to society. What is more, the nature that Goethe's writing evokes is a realm of teeming change, where order and harmony are only the grand pattern composed by constant movement, and this too he accepts—he is as far from the traditional lament over the mutability of things as he is from the more modern horror and ennui at their changeless repetition. His vision is as dynamic as the historical dialectic of Hegel or Marx (indeed it is more so, since he does not allow as they do for a stage where motion gives way to stasis). And although Goethe never applied this vision specifically to politics, and became as he aged less liberal in his overt social attitudes, what he created remains a transferable model of life which is incompatible with static conceptions. That is implied by Matthew Arnold's judgement on Goethe's 'profound imperturbable naturalism' as something 'absolutely fatal to routine thinking'; and he goes on: 'Nothing could be more really subversive of the foundations on which the old European order rested; and it may be remarked that no persons are so radically detached from this order, no persons so thoroughly modern, as those who have felt Goethe's influence most deeply.'

That judgement may seem dated at first sight. There have since been literary statements more radically subversive in obvious ways than Goethe's, many of them as canonical in unhappiness and the rejection of the human condition as he was canonical in its happy affirmation. To go along unthinkingly with these negations is part of what Lionel Trilling called the 'progressive pieties' and the routine acceptance of 'the modern self-consciousness and the modern self-pity'. Yet, as Trilling acutely discerned, such acceptance may in practice be defeatist:

> The modern self-pity is certainly not without its justification; but if the circumstances that engender it are ever to be overcome, we must sometimes wonder whether this work can be done by minds which are taught in youth to accept these sad conditions of ours as the only right objects of contemplation.

So although the contrary 'imagination of felicity' may seem at first 'a betrayal of our awareness of our world of pain' and hence, in the broadest sense, 'politically inappropriate', it may in fact be that the presentation of such a positive image is 'the poet's political duty'. In other words, a full and challenging conception of happiness and of life as it might be is a necessary complement to mere negations, a corrective to the 'shrunken' image of man's condition, and could have consequences reaching far beyond literature.

Goethe provides such a conception; and if the basis for creating it, or the consequence of creating it, was a happy life of his own, that can be seen as not just his personal good fortune but a representative human achievement, a historical mission. His work, like his life, offers a norm—he is indeed monumentally normal beside many of the developments in literature and men's thinking about literature since his time: the growing existential gloom; the social marginality of writers; the 'poètes maudits', with their deliberate deranging of the senses; the pursuers of art for its own question-begging sake; the hermetically obscure, the agonisers over how to write at all, the despairers of ever conveying thought; and most recently the dehumanisers of literature who would detach it from its roots in life and make it a self-referential game, sabotaging men's most valuable form of open communication by simplistic doubts of its viability. Beside all this, Goethe's normality is not antiquated but defiant and invigorating. He stands high above this subsequent modernity—one cannot say 'overshadowing' it, since it is not shadow that he spreads. Rather, his work is itself a happy constellation, luminous against the dark.

Note on sources

1 Joyce: *Finnegans Wake*, new ed., London 1950, p. 539.
Byron: dedication to the second edition of *Sardanapalus*, 1823.
Carlyle: *Sartor Resartus*, quoted in Rosemary Ashton, *The German Idea. Four English Writers and the Reception of German Thought 1800–1860*, Cambridge 1980, p. 19.

9 Lessing: *Briefe, die neueste Literatur betreffend*, number 51 (1759) in: *Sämtliche Schriften*, ed. Lachmann–Muncker, VIII, 140.

10 Marvell: 'The Mower against Gardens' (*c.*1640).
Petrarch: *Familiares*, Book 7, Letter iv, Nov. 1347.

12 Eliot: 'Reflections on "vers libre"' (1917), in *Selected Prose*, ed. John Hayward, Penguin Books 1953, p. 91.
Wordsworth: 'Preface to the Second Edition of "Lyrical Ballads"' (1802) in: *Works*, ed. de Selincourt, Oxford 1944, II, 393.

14 Constable: from C. R. Leslie's notes of the last lecture given by Constable, in Leslie, *Memoirs of the Life of John Constable*, repr. London 1951, p. 327.

25 Voltaire: *Lettres philosophiques* (1734), number 18.

27 Nietzsche: *Vom Nutzen und Nachteil der Historie für das Leben*, the second of the *Unzeitgemäße Betrachtungen* (1874), section 2.

39 Pater: *The Renaissance*, repr. London 1877, p. 219.

42 Auden: introduction to the Penguin Classics translation of the *Italian Journey* by Auden and Elizabeth Mayer, 1970, p. 16.

51 Heisenberg: in his last essay, 'Gedanken zur "Reise der Kunst ins Innere"', *Versuche zu Goethe. Festschrift Erich Heller*, Heidelberg 1976, p. 325.

52 Benn: prefatory note to his essay *Goethe und die Naturwissenschaften* of 1932, added for a republication in 1933 after the Nazis had taken power. See Benn, *Gesammelte Werke*, ed. Dieter Wellershoff, vol. 1, Wiesbaden ³1965, p. 614.

62 Schiller: *On the Aesthetic Education of Man*, trans. L. A. Willoughby and E. M. Wilkinson, Oxford 1967, repr. 1982, p. 47 (Letter 7).

63 Novalis: *Schriften*, ed. Kluckhohn and Samuel, Leipzig [1928], III, 314.

85 George Eliot: 'The Morality of *Wilhelm Meister*', in: *Essays of George Eliot*, ed. Thomas Pinney, New York and London 1963, pp. 146 f.

88 'has been well called': by Grete Schaeder, *Gott und Welt*, Hamlin 1947, p. 82.

89 Hegel: the section entitled 'Das Ende der romantischen Kunstform', in: *Sämtliche Werke*, ed. H. Glockner, vol. 13, Stuttgart 1928, pp. 228 ff.
Novalis: in an annotation to Friedrich Schlegel's *Ideen*, in *Schriften*, ed. cit., III, 357.

93 Freud: letter to Carl Gustav Jung, 15 June 1911, quoted in Ronald W. Clark, *Freud: The Man and the Cause*, London 1980, p. 310.

96 Nobel prizewinner: William Golding in an interview originally published in *Quarto*, Nov. 1980, and partially reprinted in The *Guardian*, Saturday 8 Oct. 1983, p. 17. It includes the statement: 'Where you have fulfilment and enhancement, you don't get a

story. There is no *story* about a happy life, there is a happy life.'

Nobel selection committee: the Swedish writer and dissenting committee-member, Artur Lundkvist, was quoted as saying of Golding: 'Of course, he is pessimistic, but that is almost a qualification for the job nowadays. An author almost has to be a pessimist' (*Observer*, 9 Oct. 1983, p. 7). Golding was apparently not pessimistic enough for Mr Lundkvist.

98 Francis Bacon: *The Advancement of Learning*, Book I, in: *The Works of Francis Bacon*, ed. Spedding, Ellis and Heath, London 1857, III, 285 f.

100 Matthew Arnold: 'Heinrich Heine' (1863), in *Essays in Criticism*, First Series, ed. R. H. Super, Michigan 1962, p. 110.

Lionel Trilling: *Beyond Culture. Essays on Literature and Learning*, repr. Peregrine Books 1967, pp. 20 f., 57 f.

Further reading

1. Translations

There is no lack of these. I list the more recent, most of them currently (1984) still in print.

POETRY. *Selected Verse*, the German text (including extracts and lyrics from *Faust I*) with prose translations by David Luke, Penguin 1964—particularly helpful for those with some German. *Selected Poems*, ed. Christopher Middleton, London 1983, German text with verse translations by various hands which (with the reservations stated in my text) make it in some measure possible to read Goethe as a poet. *Roman Elegies*, German text with a verse translation by David Luke, London 1977, captures well the tone and mood of the cycle. *Hermann und Dorothea*, German text with verse translation by Daniel Coogan, New York ²1976.

FAUST. Parts I and II (separate volumes), verse translations by Philip Wayne, Penguin Classics 1949, 1959 and frequent reprints; Parts I and II (abridged), verse translation by Louis MacNeice, London 1957; Parts I and II, prose translation by Barker Fairley, Toronto 1970; Parts I and II, verse translation by Walter Arndt, with extensive documentation on the play's genesis and selected criticism, edited by Cyrus Hamlin, New York 1976; Part I only, verse translation by Randall Jarrell, New York 1976.

OTHER DRAMAS. *Goethe's Plays*, translated by Charles E. Passage, London 1980. The major plays from this volume are also available as separate paperbacks, as are *Iphigenie* and *Tasso* in translations by John Prudhoe, Manchester 1966. John Arden's *Ironhand*, London 1965, is an interesting adaptation rather than translation of *Götz von Berlichingen*. *Egmont* is one of *Five German Tragedies*, translated by F. J. Lamport, Penguin Classics 1969.

NOVELS. There are numerous translations of *The Sufferings* [or: *Sorrows*] *of Young Werther*, e.g. by Elizabeth Mayer and Louise Bogan (together with *Novella*), New York 1973, and by B. Q. Morgan, London 1957. Similarly of *Die Wahlverwandtschaften*, either as *Elective Affinities*, the title of versions by R. J. Hollingdale, Penguin Classics 1971, and by Mayer and Bogan, Indiana 1963; or as *Kindred by Choice*, in the version by H. M. Waidson, London 1960. Waidson has also translated the complete *Wilhelm Meister* sequence (excepting the *Theatrical Mission* fragment), in six volumes, London 1977–82.

AUTOBIOGRAPHY AND DOCUMENTS. John Oxenford's translation of *Dichtung und Wahrheit* as *The Autobiography of Goethe* (1848) was reissued London 1971. *Italian Journey*, translated by W. H. Auden and Elizabeth Mayer (with occasional toning-down of Goethe's anti-religious comments) is in Penguin Classics, 1970. John Oxenford also translated Johann Peter Eckermann's *Conversations with Goethe in the Last Years of his Life*, reprinted London 1930. A selection from Eckermann and other sources is provided in *Goethe: Conversations and Encounters*, translated by David Luke and Robert Pick, London 1966. For a selection of letters, see *Letters from Goethe*, translated by M. Herzfeld and C. A. M. Sym, Edinburgh 1957.

OTHER. *Great Writings of Goethe*, ed. Stephen Spender,

New York 1958, is a short selection, drawing in part on translations listed above. *Goethe on Art*, translated and edited by John Gage, London 1980. *Botanical Writings*, translated by Bertha Mueller, ed. C. J. Engard, Honolulu 1952; *Theory of Colours*, translated by C. L. Eastlake, reprinted London 1967; *Readings in Goethean Science*, ed. Herbert H. Koepf and Linda S. Jolly, Rhode Island 1978.

2. Works on Goethe

BIOGRAPHIES. Earliest and still in many ways best is G. H. Lewes's *Life and Works of Goethe*, London 1855 and frequent reprints. Briefer and sound is J. G. Robertson's *Life*, London 1932. Richard Friedenthal's *Goethe, his Life and Times*, English translation London 1965, is a modern German view, with some of the routine modern scepticism towards past greatness. Remarkable as an imaginative reconstruction, and delightful as intellectual comedy, is Thomas Mann's novel *Lotte in Weimar* (translated by Helen Lowe-Porter, earlier entitled *The Beloved Returns*), Penguin 1968 and reprints.

CRITICAL. Inevitably, most critical work has been addressed to students of German and contains quotations in the original. But there is still much to be gained from Barker Fairley's three outstanding books, *Goethe as Revealed in his Poetry*, London 1932, *A Study of Goethe*, Oxford 1947, and *Faust: Six Essays*, Oxford 1953; as there is from the less technical of the essays in E. M. Wilkinson and L. A. Willoughby, *Goethe: Poet and Thinker*, London 1962. George Santayana's *Three Philosophical Poets: Lucretius, Dante, Goethe*, Cambridge, Mass., 1910 and several reprints, establishes the right broad framework for evaluating Goethe, although he concentrates unduly on *Faust* and says much about Lucretius's poetry which would apply equally well to

Goethe's. Ronald Peacock, *Goethe's Major Plays*, Manchester 1959, analyses these great literary works with an acute awareness of the specific conditions of drama and theatre. Eudo C. Mason's *Goethe's Faust. Its Genesis and Purport*, Berkeley and Los Angeles 1967, is a vigorous account of the complex problems of *Faust* scholarship, though Mason's own polemical arguments do not always provide ideal solutions. Goethe's major fiction is discussed by H. S. Reiss, *Goethe's Novels*, London 1969; his scientific theories by G. A. Wells, *Goethe and the Development of Science 1750–1900* Alphen 1978, and by H. B. Nisbet, *Goethe and the Scientific Tradition*, London 1972; his use of antiquity by Humphry Trevelyan, *Goethe and the Greeks*, Cambridge 1941, reprinted 1981; his links with other arts in W. D. Robson-Scott, *The Younger Goethe and the Visual Arts*, Cambridge 1981; and his thought on literature in a chapter of René Wellek's *A History of Modern Criticism 1750–1950*, vol. 1, London 1955. Georg Lukács argues a Marxist interpretation of several of the major works in *Goethe and his Age*, translated by Robert Anchor, London, 1968. A rich harvest of essays on every conceivable aspect of Goethe and his work, by British and visiting scholars, is contained in the *Publications of the English Goethe Society*, 1886–1912 and 1924 to date. Some of the arguments of the present book are given in fuller form with fuller quotation in T. J. Reed, *The Classical Centre. Goethe and Weimar 1775–1832*, London 1980.

Index

absolutism, 5, 23, 31
activity (*see also* movement), 71, 76, 78 ff.
administration, 5, 29 f., 32, 34
Aeschylus, 97
alienation, 81
amorality, 69, 71
allegory, 30, 67 f., 78
antiquity, 3, 33 ff., 35 f., 39, 41 ff., 66, 88 f., 98
architecture, 34 f., 98
Aristotle, 25, 81
Arnold, Matthew, 1, 100
Auden, W. H., 42
Augustine, St, 48
authenticity, 95

Bacon, Francis, 46, 98
Benn, Gottfried, 52
Berlichingen, Gottfried von, 26
Bildungsroman, 62
biology, 43 f., 47, 49
Blake, William, 77
botany, 31, 43 f., 45, 47 f.
bourgeois drama, 23 f., 73
bourgeoisie, 4, 23 f., 61 f., 64
Byron, Lord, 1, 29, 42, 68

Carl August, Duke of Saxe-Weimar, 5 f., 29 f.
Carlyle, Thomas, 1
Catullus, 41
Cervantes, 56
Chekhov, Anton Pavlovich, 60
Christianity, 9 f., 14, 16, 17, 36, 44, 66, 70, 72 f., 77 f., 89, 95
Classicism, 4, 5, 7, 40 ff., 54–6 82 ff., 99

Coleridge, Samuel Taylor, 1
Constable, John, 14
confessional writing, 4, 19, 22 f.

Dante, 1
Darwin, Charles, 47 f.
Diderot, Denis, 24
drama, 22–8, 57–60, 66–81, 82
Dürer, Albrecht, 32

Eckermann, Johann Peter, vi, 77
Eliot, George, 1, 85
Eliot, T.S., 12
empiricism, 6, 14, 46, 50, 71, 95
Enlightenment, 6, 16, 28, 58, 69, 78 f., 85
epistolary novel, 18
erotic poetry, 9, 41 f., 86 f.
Euripides, 57 f.
evil, 71, 78

feudalism, see absolutism
form, 4, 11 f., 61, 65
Frederick the Great, 23
'free verse', 12
French culture: influence of, 23 f.; influence on, 3
French Revolution, 5, 64, 82 f., 90
Freud, Sigmund, 93

genesis, 23, 67, 71, 73
geology, 31, 44, 82
Goethe, Johann Caspar (father), 4
GOETHE, Johann Wolfgang: sketch of life, 4–7;
WORKS:
  Achilleis, 83
  Campaign in France, 90

Index

Chinese–German Days and Seasons, 89
correspondence with Schiller, 56
Diary of the Italian Journey, 33 ff.
Dichtung und Wahrheit, see *Poetry and Truth*
Egmont, 28, 57
Elective Affinities, 73, 84 ff., 87
Faust, 1, 7, 8, 22 f., 65, 66–81, 82, 89
Faust, a Fragment, 66
French Revolution, dramas about, 82
Götz von Berlichingen, 25 ff., 29
Hermann and Dorothea, 64
Iphigenie in Tauris, 29, 57 ff., 69, 85
Italian Journey, 90
Novella, 87
Poetry: early poems, 10 ff.; first Weimar poems, 29 f.; Classical poems, 40 ff., 47, 63 f.; late poems, 88, 92 f.
Poetry and Truth, 4, 7, 13, 90, 94
Roman Elegies, 40 ff., 88
Sufferings of Young Werther, 5, 17–22, 29, 64, 90, 94, 98
'The Diary', 86 f.
Torquato Tasso, 57, 60, 63, 90
Trilogy of Passion, 3, 90
West-eastern Divan, 88 f.
Wilhelm Meister's Apprenticeship, 57, 61 ff., 85
Wilhelm Meister's Theatrical Mission, 57, 61
Wilhelm Meister's Years of Travel, 87 f.
Wahlverwandtschaften, Die (see *Elective Affinities*)
Goethe, Katharina Elisabeth, *née* Textor (mother), 4 f.
Golding, William, 96
Great Chain of Being, 44

Hafiz, 88
happiness, 5, 14, 16, 21, 94, 96 ff., 101
Hegel, Georg Wilhelm Friedrich, 79, 81, 89, 100
Heisenberg, Werner, 51
Herder, Johann Gottfried, 6, 13 f., 24, 27
historism, 24
Holy Roman Empire, 24, 26
Homer, 13, 64, 83
Hume, David, 16, 19

Ibsen, Henrik, 97
idyll, 5, 15, 20, 64, 75, 96
individualism, 10 f., 14 f., 17, 22, 28, 54, 56, 64, 80, 85, 95
Industrial Revolution, 80 f.
inspiration, 2, 13, 29 f., 65
Italy, 5, 32–40, 57, 98

Jerusalem, Carl Wilhelm, 17 ff.
Joyce, James, 1, 68

Kafka, Franz, 97
Kant, Immanuel, 60, 78, 87, 98
Kestner, Charlotte, *née* Buff, 19
Kestner, Johann Christian, 19
Klopstock, Friedrich Gottlieb, 9 f., 14

Lavater, Johann Kaspar, 95, 97 f.
Lawrence, D. H., 41
Leibniz, Gottfried Wilhelm, 44
Lessing, Gotthold Ephraim, 9, 39
Linnaeus, Carl, 44, 49
Lucretius, 52
Luther, Martin, 8

Marlowe, Christopher, 66
Marvell, Andrew, 10
Marx, Karl, 81, 100
mathematics, 49
melancholy, 20 f.
metamorphosis, 47, 92
Metternich, Clemens, Prince, 6

Michelangelo, 34
Molière, 56
monism, 37
Montaigne, Michel Eyquem, sieur de, 33
morality, 4, 59, 62, 71, 78 f., 83, 84 f.
morphology, 44, 48, 92
Möser, Justus, 24
movement (*see also* activity), 15, 53, 71, 75, 77, 81, 82, 92
Mozart, Wolfgang Amadeus, 58
myth, mythology, 12, 34, 66 ff., 75, 78, 83, 88, 90

Napoleon, 5 f., 88
nation, nationalism, 24 f., 27 f.
nature, 10, 12, 15 f., 20 f., 25 f., 30, 32, 34, 36 f., 38 f., 44 f., 55 f., 60 f., 63 f., 78 f., 84 f., 86 f., 91, 95, 100
Nazism, 52
Neo-classicism, 23, 25, 27
Newton, Isaac, 49, 52
Nietzsche, Friedrich Wilhelm, 27
nihilism, 20, 94
Novalis, 63, 89

objectivity, 18, 34 f., 40, 60, 97 f.
'occasional' poetry, 11
optimism, 6, 16, 17, 94 ff., 99 f.
organic growth, 13, 36, 37 f., 83 f.
Ossian, 13

Palladio, Andrea, 34, 36 f.
pantheism, 15, 69
Pater, Walter, 39
perception, 14, 25 f., 34 f., 40, 43, 95, 97, 98 f.
pessimism, 17, 22, 95 ff.
Petrarch, 10
physics, 49 f., 53
Pindar, 14
Plato, 47
poetry, eighteenth-century, 9
politics, 6, 28, 82 f., 99 f.

Propertius, 41
Pushkin, Aleksandr Sergeevich, 8

radical evil, 78
Raphael, 34, 36
religion, 83, 88 f.
Reni, Guido, 38
representation, 10 f., 25 f., 39
Richardson, Samuel, 18
rococo, 9, 87
Romanticism: 8 f., 16, 54, 98 f.; English, 1; German, 7, 63, 85, 89, 90
Rousseau, Jean-Jacques, 16, 18, 55, 100

Schiller, Johann Christoph Friedrich, 4, 6 f., 51, 55 f., 57, 62, 64, 66, 83, 91
science, 3, 6, 31 f., 36 f., 43–53, 92 f., 95
Scott, Sir Walter, 1, 27
secularism, 6, 14 f.
self-realisation, 32, 37 f., 61
Shakespeare, William, 1, 8, 13, 25 ff., 31, 56 f., 67, 91
specialisation, 51, 61
Spinoza, Baruch, 45 f.
Stein, Charlotte von, 30, 32, 45
'Sturm und Drang', 29 f.
suicide, 19 f.
symbol, symbolism, 47, 76 f., 85 f., 87, 88 f.

Tamburlaine, 88
theatre, 23 ff., 61 f.
Tibullus, 41
Tintoretto, 38
Tischbein, Johann Heinrich, 36
Tolstoy, Lev Nikolaevich, 97
tragedy, 17, 22, 57, 60, 72 ff., 94, 96
Trilling, Lionel, 101

Urphänomen (*Urpflanze*), 46 f., 49 f.

Index

Viq d'Azyr, 45
Voltaire, 25, 63
Vulcanism, 82
Vulpius, Christiane, 6, 40, 43

Wars, French Revolutionary, Napoleonic, 5 f., 31, 64, 83, 88
wholeness: of man, 43, 50, 61 f., 98; of observed phenomena, 44 f., 50, 92
Winckelmann, Johann Joachim, 33
wisdom, 1, 3, 79, 87 ff., 91, 94
Wordsworth, William, 12 f.

Zelter, Karl Friedrich, 94